El Salvador
the people and culture

Greg Nickles

A Bobbie Kalman Book
The Lands, Peoples, and Cultures Series

Crabtree Publishing Company
www.crabtreebooks.com

The Lands, Peoples, and Cultures Series

Created by Bobbie Kalman

Coordinating editor
Ellen Rodger

Assistant editor
P.A. Finlay

Production coordinator
Rosie Gowsell

Project development, photo research, and design
First Folio Resource Group, Inc.
  Erinn Banting
  Tom Dart
  Söğüt Y. Güleç
  Alana Lai
  Debbie Smith

Editing
Carolyn Black

Separations and film
Embassy Graphics

Printer
Worzalla Publishing Company

Consultants
Elisa de Carranza, Consulate General of El Salvador, Houston; Ana Cecilia Romero and Patricia Zepeda, Consulate of El Salvador, Toronto

Photographs
AP/Wide World Photo: p. 24 (left), p. 26, p. 27 (right); Piers Cavendish/Impact: p. 22 (left); Corbis/Magma Photo News Inc./Bettmann: p. 8, p. 9 (left), p. 13 (right); Corbis/Magma Photo News Inc./Joel W. Rogers: p. 9 (right); J.P. Courau/DDB Stock Photo: p. 12 (bottom), p. 24 (right), Lizzette Marenco de Dreyfus: p. 12 (top); Max Dreyfus: p. 16 (right); Carl Frank/Photo Researchers: p. 17 (bottom); Carlos Henriquez: p. 14 (left), p. 29; Mike Hutchison: p. 27 (left), p. 30 (top); Greg Johnston: cover, p. 10 (bottom), p. 20 (left); Alison M. Jones: p. 6 (left), p. 13 (left), p. 21 (bottom), p. 23 (both), p. 30 (bottom); Alyx Kellington/DDB Stock Photo: title page; North Wind Pictures: p. 6 (right),p. 7; Reuters/Luis Galdamez/Archive Photos: p. 15; Sean Sprague/Panos Pictures: p. 11 (both), p. 14 (right), p. 28 (left), p. 31; Tayacan/Panos Pictures: p. 22 (right); Anneke van Gijzen: p. 3, p. 19 (top), p. 28 (right); Eric Velado: p. 10 (top), p. 16 (left), p. 17 (top), p. 18, p. 19 (bottom), p. 20 (right), p. 21 (top), p. 25

Illustrations
Sylvie Bourbonnière, Anna Goodson Management: pp. 4–5
Dianne Eastman: icon
David Wysotski, Allure Illustrations: back cover

Cover: A boy holds up a bundle of lobsters and crabs from an outdoor fish market in La Libertad, in southern El Salvador.

Title page: A girl sits in a market stall where her family sells spices, noodles, and rice.

Icon: A *marimba*, which is a type of xylophone that has keys made from hollow gourds, appears at the head of each section.

Back cover: The *tigrillo*, or ocelot, is a small wildcat that lives in the mountainous regions of El Salvador.

Published by
Crabtree Publishing Company

PMB 16A,
350 Fifth Avenue
Suite 3308
New York
N.Y. 10118

612 Welland Avenue
St. Catharines
Ontario, Canada
L2M 5V6

73 Lime Walk
Headington
Oxford OX3 7AD
United Kingdom

Cataloging in Publication Data

Nickles, Greg, 1969-
  El Salvador. The people and culture / Greg Nickles.
    p. cm. -- (The lands, peoples, and cultures series)
    Includes index.
  Summary: Introduces the religion, holidays and festivals, art, traditional and modern dance and music, language, and literature of El Salvador.
    ISBN 0-7787-9368-0 (RLB) -- ISBN 0-7787-9736-8 (pbk.)
  1. El Salvador--Social life and customs--21st century--Juvenile literature. 2. El Salvador--History--Juvenile literature. [1. El Salvador--Social life and customs.] I. Title. II. Series
  F1488.5 .N53 2002
  972.8405'2--dc21
                                        2001032530
                                        LC

Contents

A tale of the first human

Long ago, the ancient Mayan people lived in El Salvador. They told a story of a time when only plants and wild animals lived on the earth. The supreme being, Hunabku, and the other Mayan gods watched over these plants and animals. One day, the gods commanded the animals, "Call out our names and **worship** us, your creators and **ancestors**." The animals could only reply with noisy squawks, roars, growls, and honks.

"This is not good," Hunabku said to the other gods. "We must have creatures on this earth that can think and speak, so they can honor and serve us." All day and night, the gods debated how to make such creatures. Finally, the supreme Hunabku said, "Quickly, let us build our new creatures out of dirt before the magical hour of dawn arrives."

The gods finished making the dirt creatures at sunrise, and commanded, "Call out our names and worship us, your creators and ancestors." The dirt creatures spoke, but their words made no sense. Later, when it started to rain, the creatures turned into mud and were washed away.

"We must try our luck again," said mighty Hunabku. He asked the gods Ixpiyacoc and Ixmucané, the grandparents of **humanity**, for advice. They replied, "Why not make the creatures from wood?"

The gods worked all night. As the next day dawned, their skinny wooden creatures came to life. The gods grew excited watching them chatter and climb trees. "Call out our names and worship us," they commanded, but the creatures did not obey. Instead, they ran away to live with the other wild animals. Today, we call these creatures monkeys.

The gods were disappointed, but Hunabku encouraged them. "These creatures are much better than the ones we made from mud. With the knowledge we gained making them, we will finally build the creature we want."

Then, Hunabku said to Ah Mun, the god of corn, "Give me a tiny, golden kernel of corn." From the kernel, the gods very carefully molded another creation, which came to life at sunrise. This time, the creature moved, talked, and thought. When the gods commanded, it spoke their names and worshiped them. At last, Hunabku and the other gods were satisfied. Hunabku announced proudly, "We have created the first human on earth."

From empires to independence

The Mayan ruins at San Andrés are decorated with intricate carvings that depict gods and goddesses, ancient leaders, and powerful warriors.

Many peoples have lived in El Salvador throughout the land's long history. The Olmec people built the first known civilization there 3,000 years ago. They created cities of stone that had large **step pyramids** and monumental sculptures. The Mayan people lived in El Salvador after the Olmecs. The Maya made important discoveries in writing, mathematics, and **astronomy**, and created very precise calendars. About 1,000 years ago, the Pipíl settled in El Salvador. They were skilled warriors who, like the Maya, knew a great deal about science and stone building.

During the 1500s, Don Pedro de Alvarado conquered Mexico and much of Central America, including present-day Guatemala, El Salvador, and Honduras.

Conquest by Spain

The Spanish conquest began in El Salvador in 1524. Spanish soldiers, called *conquistadores,* arrived in sailing ships from Europe. They conquered the peoples they found and made them **subjects** and slaves of Spain. The Spaniards' ships, horses, steel armor, and weapons made them stronger warriors than El Salvador's Native peoples. By 1528, the leader of the *conquistadores* in El Salvador, Don Pedro de Alvarado, conquered the Pipíl.

In the name of the savior

After the conquest, El Salvador and other places in Central America became part of a Spanish province called Guatemala. Spanish settlers and merchants came to the province, bringing their culture and the Christian religion. Christians follow the teachings of Jesus Christ, whom they believe is the son of God and whom they call their **savior**. Spanish settlers used their word for savior, *salvador*, to name the region of El Salvador and its future **capital**, San Salvador.

Toward independence

Under Spanish rule, El Salvador's economy became based on agriculture. A few wealthy families who were originally from Spain established large farms, called **plantations**, where they grew sugar and **indigo**. These families also helped govern the province.

After nearly 300 years, the wealthy families wanted to rule Central America on their own, without Spain's help. Many workers and other local people also supported **independence** from Spain because they hoped it would improve their living conditions. Spain refused to grant their wish. In 1811, Salvadorans José Matías Delgado and his nephew Manuel José Arce began a **rebellion** against Spanish rule. The rebellion was soon crushed, but Delgado and Arce became heroes.

New countries

In 1821, the province of Guatemala broke away from Spain. Two years later, El Salvador, along with four other Central American countries, became part of the United Provinces of Central America. Political and religious differences soon divided the people of the United Provinces, and **civil war** erupted in 1827. The war ended in 1829, but the problems continued. The United Provinces broke apart in 1840, and El Salvador became its own country in 1841.

Native peoples fight back

Spanish rule greatly affected the Native peoples of El Salvador. Thousands died while fighting the Spanish during and after the conquest or while working as slaves on plantations. Others died of European diseases. The Spanish forced the remaining Native peoples to adopt the Spanish language and culture.

Salvadoran Anastasio Aquino led the Native peoples in a rebellion against the Spanish in 1833. Many non-Native people, tired of living in poverty, also fought in the rebellion. The rebels won the cities of Zacatecoluca and San Vicente, in the central part of the country, but government troops defeated them in the mountains. Aquino was put to death for treason, or crimes against his country. Today, many Salvadorans remember him as a great hero.

Struggle and civil war

Throughout the 1800s, wealthy Salvadoran families controlled El Salvador's government. By forcing small farmers out of business, they took over most of the country's farmland for their plantations. The *Catorce Familias*, or "Fourteen Families," became the most powerful people in the land. They made large fortunes growing and selling coffee beans and cotton.

Coming together

Increasingly, Salvadorans relied on the plantations for jobs. These jobs involved hard work, but the workers were not paid well. They began to blame the *Catorce Familias*. Some argued that **fertile** land should be taken away from the wealthy and given to the workers. Others took part in violent attacks to force the government to make changes.

In this photograph from 1931, people shop in a busy market in San Salvador.

Years of troubles

In 1929, a worldwide economic crisis, called the Great Depression, began. Thousands of Salvadorans lost their jobs because other countries stopped buying their crops. Led by **revolutionaries** such as Augustín Farabundo Martí, many Salvadorans rebelled against the government. The Salvadoran military took control of the country in 1931, partly to protect the *Catorce Familias*. The government ordered a massacre, later called *la matanza* or "the slaughter," to wipe out the rebels and their supporters. Up to 30,000 Salvadorans, mostly Native peoples, were murdered. Martí was executed, and surviving rebels went into hiding.

Military rule

Military leaders controlled El Salvador for most of the next 50 years. Although they encouraged new industries, many Salvadorans still suffered shortages of food, housing, and jobs.

The Soccer War

In 1969, El Salvador went to war with its neighbor Honduras. The conflict was called the Soccer War because it began right after the two countries played against each other in the World Cup soccer tournament. They fought the Soccer War over Salvadorans who had moved illegally into Honduras to find a better life. Honduras wanted El Salvador to take back the illegal **immigrants.** During the war's four days of heavy fighting, several thousand people were killed or injured.

The civil war

Since *la matanza*, rebels in El Salvador continued to plot against the government. In the 1970s, they formed a new army called the FMLN, or *Farabundo Martí Liberation National*. The FMLN pledged to take over the country, and end poverty and government corruption. They kidnapped members of the government and military, and held them for **ransom** to get money for their own army. They also killed hundreds of people who refused to support them. The government forces, in turn, killed many peasant supporters of the FMLN. In 1979, the conflict between the government and the FMLN erupted into civil war, during which tens of thousands of people were arrested, tortured, and killed.

A soldier fighting during the civil war carries his wounded friend to safer ground.

Americans protest against their government's military and financial support of the Salvadoran government's fight against FMLN rebels.

Peace at last

Slowly, the rebels' actions led to change. In 1983, El Salvador adopted a new constitution. One year later, elected politicians replaced military rulers. José Napoleón Duarte became president. In 1992, the government signed a peace agreement with the FMLN. The agreement promised that the poor would get land and FMLN members would help run the country. During the long war, over 75,000 people were killed and over one million fled to other countries for safety.

Building new lives

Today, millions of Salvadorans are grateful for the peace they have enjoyed since 1992. They are slowly rebuilding their country. Salvadorans hope that their leaders will keep the peace and make changes to improve their daily lives.

The Salvadorans

More than six million people live in El Salvador, although geographically it is the smallest country in Central America. It is one of the most densely populated countries in the world. Most Salvadorans crowd into cities and towns on the plains and highlands. Few people live in the mountainous countryside.

Both Spanish and Native

Many Spaniards who settled in El Salvador in the 1500s **intermarried** and had children with Native peoples. Today, more than 90 percent of El Salvador's population has mixed Spanish and Native ancestry. They speak Spanish and follow many Spanish traditions.

Dressed in a brightly colored headscarf and dress, a woman prepares to perform a traditional dance during a festival in Suchitoto, in central El Salvador.

Pineapples, coconuts, bananas, and other fresh fruit are for sale at this farmer's market in San Vicente, in central El Salvador.

A young boy plays on a dock near his family's boat in La Libertad, on the southern coast.

From Europe and the Middle East

A small number of Salvadorans have solely Spanish ancestry. These people usually belong to the country's wealthy families and make up two to five percent of the population. Another small number of Salvadorans are descendants of Palestinian, Jewish, and Lebanese immigrants who came to the country in the 1800s.

Native peoples

People estimate that around 60,000 Native people live in El Salvador, although no one is sure of the exact number. The reason for this uncertainty is that many Native peoples look similar to other Salvadorans. They have also adopted the Spanish language, styles of clothing, and customs, hoping to escape poor treatment and violence from other Salvadorans.

Pipíl survivors

Of the remaining groups of Native peoples in El Salvador, the Pipíl are the largest. The Pipíl live mainly in villages in the southwest part of the country, where they still preserve some of their culture. Some Pipíl continue to believe in their traditional gods of corn, rain, sun, wind, and earth. Others combine these beliefs with Christianity. They do traditional crafts such as weaving, pottery, and metalwork. Most Pipíl speak Spanish, but a few elders speak the Pipíl language, Nahuatl.

The Lenca people of eastern El Salvador are **descendants** of the ancient Maya. Little is known of the Lencas' traditions, which have nearly disappeared.

Salvadorans in other countries

Even though the civil war ended in 1992, many Salvadorans who fled the fighting remain in other countries. There, they have found jobs and homes. Many send money to their relatives in El Salvador to help them pay for food, clothes, and shelter.

A sister and brother visit their grandfather on his farm near San Salvador. About 30 percent of Salvadorans are farmers.

Religion and worship

Religion has always been an important part of community life in El Salvador. Prayer comforts worshipers, especially during the country's hard times. Sometimes, churches offer basic medical care, food, and clothing to people who do not have much money. They also help set up housing developments and craft shops where many Salvadorans live and work.

The Christian religion

Almost all Salvadorans are Christians. Their religion is based on the teachings of Jesus Christ and on the holy book called the Bible. Christians believe that Christ performed miracles such as healing the sick and returning to life after he was crucified, or put to death on a cross.

(left) Small ceramic statues and paintings depicting saints are sold outside a church in Sonsonate, in western El Salvador.

(below) The cathedral in Santa Ana, in western El Salvador, was built in 1905. It is one of the oldest Roman Catholic churches in the country.

Many of El Salvador's towns and villages have small stone churches where people gather and pray.

Catholics and Protestants

Most Salvadorans are Roman Catholics. Roman Catholicism is a **denomination** of Christianity that is about 2,000 years old. The Spanish introduced Roman Catholicism to El Salvador in the 1500s. In each town and city, they built churches and **shrines** devoted to saints, or holy people.

After the 1980s, another denomination of Christianity called Protestantism became popular. Most Salvadoran Protestants are former Roman Catholics.

Politics and poverty

Many Salvadoran religious leaders have been active in politics. Some have led people to organize themselves in their fight against poverty. This teaching began in the late 1960s and is called "liberation theology." Rather than watch silently as innocent Salvadorans were arrested and killed by the military during the civil war, Roman Catholic priests and nuns spoke out against the government. In response, the military killed many of them.

Archbishop Romero

In 1977, Oscar Anulfo Romero (1917–1980) became San Salvador's **archbishop**. Romero knew the military government committed crimes against innocent Salvadorans. He decided to take a stand after the government killed his friend, the priest Retulio Grande. Romero began publishing the names of people who had "disappeared," or were secretly arrested by the police. He also preached against violence to his followers each Sunday, urging government soldiers not to kill. As people around the world heard of the suffering in El Salvador, Romero became known as "the voice of the voiceless."

Romero's actions earned him powerful enemies. In 1980, he was murdered while leading a Sunday church service. At his funeral, many of his followers were shot and killed. Most people believe that the military sent the murderers, who were never caught. Today, Archbishop Romero is the country's most beloved hero. The Catholic Church is in the process of canonizing him, or making him a saint.

Holidays and festivals

On May 6, people in the town of Panchimalco, in central El Salvador, celebrate **Las Palmas. Las Palmas** is a festival that honors the Virgen de Fatima, a saint who is believed to have performed many miracles.

Salvadorans have many holidays and festivals. Most are religious events. Others celebrate the harvest, the anniversary of an important day in history, or the arts. Costumes, parades, sports, concerts, and dancing are all part of the festivities.

La Navidad

Christians in El Salvador celebrate the birth of Jesus Christ with *La Navidad*, or Christmas, on December 25. In the days leading up to *La Navidad*, they set up *nacimientos*, or Nativity scenes, in churches and homes. *Nacimientos* show the baby Jesus and his parents, Mary and Joseph, in the stable where Jesus was born.

La Noche Buena

On *La Noche Buena*, "The Good Night" before *La Navidad*, families go to church. There, they sing carols and watch the children's Christmas **pageant**. Then, everyone returns home for a party. Children enjoy the feasting, music, and dancing, but are anxious to go to bed so *El Niño Dios*, the baby Jesus, can bring them a present. They awake later that night or early in the morning to find a small gift under their pillow. *La Navidad* is a quiet day for families to relax and, often, to go to the beach. Children receive gifts again on January 6, the Epiphany. This holiday marks the visit of three kings who brought gifts for the baby Jesus.

Beginning December 15, special parades called **posadas** *re-enact the journey to the stable where Jesus was born. Children walk through their town or neighborhood carrying images of Mary and Joseph, stopping at each house to sing carols to the* **nacimientos.** *The* **posada** *grows larger until it reaches the last house, where everyone stays for a party.*

Honoring Christ's death

The Christian holiday of *Pascua*, or Easter, falls in March or April. *Pascua* marks the death and **resurrection** of Christ. On Good Friday, the day that Christ died, Salvadorans join in a solemn procession to church, carrying a painting or statue of Christ. At church, the priest leads songs and prayers. Then, worshipers light candles and guard a statue of Christ until nightfall.

Returning to life

On Easter Sunday, the day when Christ rose from the dead, a joyful procession carries an image of the risen Christ through the streets. The priest leads a special service, blessing Christ's followers and sometimes their animals. At home, children hunt for eggs and treats. A favorite trick is to cut the top off a raw egg, pour out the yolk, fill the egg with confetti, and then crack it over someone's head as a surprise. *Pascua* ends with feasting and parties.

Palm Sunday falls one week before Easter Sunday. Worshipers carrying palm branches blessed by the priest march in a procession with a statue of Christ.

San Miguel's *fiesta*

Every city, town, and village in El Salvador holds its own annual *fiesta*, or festival, to honor its patron saint. Roman Catholics believe that their patron saint protects them. A major focus of the *fiesta* in San Miguel, in eastern El Salvador, is a statue of its patron saint, Nuestra Señora de la Paz. The people of San Miguel believe this statue saved the city from an eruption of the nearby Chaparrastique volcano in 1787. The residents placed the statue at the door of their **cathedral** during the eruption and prayed for protection. The city was not destroyed, and residents have celebrated their *fiesta* ever since.

El Quince de Septiembre

Each year, Salvadorans and other Central Americans celebrate their independence from Spain on *El Quince de Septiembre*, or "The Fifteenth of September." In the week before this holiday, school children paint portraits and sing songs about the revolution against Spain. Then, on September 15, they parade through the streets with school marching bands. Soldiers march beside tanks; planes and helicopters fly overhead; and politicians give patriotic speeches.

Day of the Dead

In San Salvador, children celebrate Halloween on October 31 by going from door to door saying, "*Queremos dulces*," or "We want candy," and by throwing eggs. The next day, they must clean up the mess they made! November 1 marks *El Día de los Muertos*, or "The Day of the Dead." People say that the spirits of dead loved ones return to earth on that day, so it is important for families to tidy their loved ones' graves. People leave gifts of flowers on the graves and eat special honey and corn flour cakes called *hoguelas de maiz* while visiting the cemetery.

Family traditions

Folk beliefs

Salvadorans have many folk beliefs surrounding the care of both a new baby and his or her mother. For example, neither the baby nor the mother is supposed to leave home for 40 days after the birth, for fear that they will become ill.

Some people believe that a father should hold his baby when he comes home from work. If he forgets, the baby may develop a nasty case of *pujos*, or hiccups! To prevent this, the father runs outside to work up a sweat. When he comes home, he holds the baby so it feels his sweat. People believe that the sweat keeps the baby from becoming ill.

The *curandera*

In the countryside and occasionally in cities, people sometimes take sick children to a *curandera*, a woman who practices a kind of folk medicine called *brujería*. The *curandera*'s cure may involve holding the child upside down by his or her feet, or rubbing a paste of garlic on the child's body.

Cousins wait for one of the many rides at a carnival in San Salvador to begin.

The bonds between Salvadoran children, parents, grandparents, aunts, uncles, and cousins are very strong. Many relatives live together, all doing chores and taking care of one another. Families also celebrate special occasions, such as births and birthdays, with one another, enjoying large meals, music, and dancing.

A new baby

Christian families welcome a new baby into their religion with a baptism. In a baptism ceremony, holy water is sprinkled on a baby's head. While some baptisms occur at church, many others take place at home, where the family holds a large party afterward. The parents choose *padrinos*, or godparents, for their child. The *padrinos* are usually family friends who promise to help take care of the child and his or her religious education.

During Roman Catholic services, people take communion. Children make their First Communion when they are seven or eight years old.

Happy birthday!

Salvadorans make sure that birthdays start off on a happy note. Family members often rise early in the morning, so they can wake the birthday person with a loud chorus of "Happy Birthday." A band is sometimes hired to play along. Later that day, family and friends throw a party with sandwiches, cake, and dancing. At a child's party, children put on a blindfold and take turns trying to burst a *piñata* with a stick. A *piñata* is a **papier-mâché** animal that is hung in the air. Once the *piñata* bursts open, candies stored inside fall to the ground. Everyone scrambles to pick them up.

Reaching fifteen

When a Salvadoran girl turns fifteen years old, she celebrates her *quinceañera*. This party marks her passage into adulthood. She wears a special dress for the occasion. Accompanied by fourteen girlfriends, she goes to church for a ceremony in which she offers thanks for reaching adulthood. Afterward, her family holds a party and a dance.

Family and friends at a birthday party gather around a house that the children made as a gift.

Elisa's arms are getting tired from carrying these watermelons home from the market. Watermelons are a favorite treat at birthday parties.

Music and dance

Across El Salvador, dance and music are important at home, at church, and during celebrations. Many people, especially in the countryside, enjoy traditional styles of dance and music. In towns and cities, rock and salsa music are popular. The country's symphony orchestra, *La Orquesta Simfónica de El Salvador*, performs classical music.

Very old instruments

Archaeologists, digging in the ruins of ancient Salvadoran settlements, uncovered many types of instruments that folk musicians still play today. These include *pitos*, which are high-pitched whistles, *chirimías* pipes, and drums such as the large, booming *tambor* and the smaller, tapping *tun*.

Strings and percussion

People from other countries introduced many instruments that Salvadoran musicians now play. Spanish settlers introduced the guitar, which became one of the most important instruments in Salvadoran folk music.

Another common folk instrument, the *marimba*, is like a wooden xylophone. The keys of a *marimba* are made from hollow **gourds**. A musician strikes the gourds using a padded stick to make a chiming sound. Usually, only one person plays a *marimba*, but some *marimbas* are so large that nine musicians can play them at once!

A *marimba* festival

Each year, San Miguel holds a festival to celebrate *marimba* music. The festival lasts several days. Bands with *marimbas* and other instruments perform on the city's main streets. Crowds of people gather around to listen and dance.

Children play different traditional instruments, such as **castanets**, *which are clapped together with the thumb and fingers;* **maracas**, *which are shaken;* **marimbas**; *and a* **tambor**.

Two girls, dressed in fancy costumes, perform a traditional dance for their classmates at a school assembly.

Singing *canciónes*

Canción is Spanish for "song." *Canciónes* are one of the most common types of folk music performed in El Salvador. Traditional *canciónes* describe Salvadorans' daily lives or tell about important events that took place in the country. Many *canciónes* are funny songs or songs of love. Singers perform *canciónes* at home with family and friends, or at public events, where everyone is invited to sing along.

Traditional dances

Salvadorans perform traditional dances at festivals or parties. The traditional *cúmbia* has short, sliding steps that are danced to the fast rhythm of *cúmbia* music. Other traditional dances come from the rain dances of the ancient Mayan people.

"El Carbonero," or "the charcoal man," is a popular traditional dance in El Salvador. People dance around a knife, called la cuma, that workers use to cut charcoal into pieces and a sack that people use to carry charcoal to the market.

Arts and crafts

Salvadorans create a wide range of handicrafts and folk art, from everyday tools and furniture to clothing, blankets, and toys. They decorate this art in both Native and Spanish styles, with bright colors and patterns.

Making handicrafts

It is not unusual for all the **artisans** of one village to make the same kind of handicraft. The village of Concepción Quezaltepeque, in the north, is a hammock-making center. Artisans in Sesuntepeque, in the central part of the country, specialize in weaving palm-leaf hats. **Wicker** workshops line the main street of Nahuizalco, in the west. Rope, pottery, fabrics, jewelry, and hand-painted crosses and cards are other products that an artisan may make. Artisans take their products to the market in the nearest town or city to sell or trade them for other goods.

A woman holds up a brightly colored woven blanket that was made in Panchimalco.

A woman carefully paints a Mayan symbol on a ceramic mug. The Maya used combinations of symbols depicting animals and people to represent different words.

Sorpresas

Salvadorans enjoy making small *sorpresas*, or "surprises." These beautiful handicrafts are a specialty of the town of Ilobasco, in the country's east. *Sorpresas* are shaped like eggs or walnuts. They open to reveal a surprise called a *típica*. The *típica* is a little scene of daily village life, made of tiny clay figures. Many girls over the age of twelve go to classes to learn how to paint *sorpresas*.

Working together

In many places, artisans' workshops are cooperatives. Cooperatives are businesses owned by all the workers. The workers share equally in any decisions and profits that are made. Cooperatives have improved the lives of many Salvadorans. Workers earn money while learning new skills.

Painting and drawing

El Salvador's artists often use traditional colors, patterns, and ideas in their work. The art of Fernando Llort (1949–) is famous around the world. Born in San Salvador, Llort moved to the northern village of La Palma in 1972. There, he began painting childlike, colorful scenes of villages, people, animals, and *campesinos*, or images of Christ. He set up a cooperative workshop, where he taught local people to paint in his style. The artwork of Llort's cooperative grew so popular that, today, most of La Palma's residents make their living from it. They closely follow Llort's style, painting images on everything from crosses to key rings.

Art and politics

Before and during the civil war, some Salvadoran artists created pieces of art that criticized the government and its military rulers. Revolutionary posters, banners, and graffiti became a common sight on the streets of Salvadoran cities. After the war, new posters gradually covered the wartime art. Politics is still an important subject of Salvadoran art.

Fernando Llort works on one of his paintings at his studio in La Palma. Today, more than 3,000 artisans in La Palma paint in Llort's style.

A brightly colored mural showing a scene from the countryside decorates the side of this home.

21

Life in the countryside

Carts pulled by bulls are used to transport water from a well to a village near San Miguel.

In a village

A *plaza* is often at the center of a village. A *plaza* is an open square lined with trees and benches. People meet there to relax with family and friends, or to take part in community events. A church usually stands beside the *plaza*, with a school nearby. Houses cluster around the center of the village.

The smallest villages have just a few houses and no churches or schools. A traveling priest goes from village to village, performing religious ceremonies for the people who live there. For special events, such as baptisms and weddings, the priest may perform services for many families at the same time. If there is no school in a village, children may walk far distances to attend classes in a neighboring village. Some children stay home to work.

Working in the fields

Many people from the countryside work on plantations. They spend long hours growing and harvesting the landowners' crops, especially coffee, for little pay. At harvest time, everyone, from children to grandparents, works in the fields. Other farmers, called subsistence farmers, tend their own land, barely growing enough to feed themselves and their families.

Children practice their spelling at a school in Suchitoto. In the countryside, many children have their classes outside.

In many ways, life in El Salvador's countryside is the same as it has been for a hundred years. Large families often live together in small homes. Most families in the countryside do not have vehicles, indoor plumbing, or electricity. More Salvadorans live in the countryside than in the city.

Under the volcano

Some families live on farms and in small communities on the slopes of El Salvador's mountains and volcanoes. Unpaved roads connect these farms and villages to surrounding towns and cities. People travel on foot, by bicycle or mule, or in a cart drawn by horses, oxen, or other farm animals. If they are traveling long distances, people usually take a bus.

The roof of this couple's home, in La Libertad, is made from red tiles.

Country homes

Farmers and other workers in the countryside often live in small houses built from wood or from sun-dried bricks made of clay and straw. Roofs are made of **thatch** or red tiles. A *choza* or *rancho*, made of branches woven together, is another common type of home. A protective layer of dried mud covers its walls. Inside the home are a few pieces of furniture. Hanging blankets, instead of walls, often divide one or two rooms. Light comes from oil lamps or candles. Outside, people cook in wood-burning ovens. They get water from a nearby well or stream, where they also bathe and wash clothes. They love listening to the radio and watching television, which they power with car batteries.

The few wealthy landowners in El Salvador live in *villas*, or estates filled with every convenience and luxury. Some of these houses are very old. Others are similar to new mansions in North America.

Many families in small villages wash their clothes in nearby rivers and streams.

El Salvador's cities are busy with people, special events, businesses, and interesting things to see. The cities are very crowded, especially San Salvador, and there are not enough homes for everyone. Despite this housing shortage, people continue to move to cities from the countryside. They are searching for better schools, hospitals, and jobs.

City homes

Families in the city have fewer children than those in the countryside. Most people live in apartment buildings or small, simple houses with basic appliances and a few pieces of furniture. The wealthiest families live in expensive neighborhoods, in luxurious homes with pools and gardens.

Traffic is backed up along a street in San Salvador, El Salvador's busy capital.

*Santa Ana's city hall, like most of the city's important buildings, stands in the central **plaza**.*

On the outskirts

Hundreds of thousands of people live on the outskirts of cities. They make their homes in older buildings or single-room houses built from cement blocks and scraps of lumber, plastic, or cardboard. Most do not have electricity, but some people hook wires into nearby city power lines. They get water from a faucet in the street, which the neighbors share.

Work and play

People in cities have many different jobs. Some work in factories or on construction sites. Others work in government offices, stores, restaurants, or hotels. After a long day, they are ready to relax and have fun. They get together with family and friends to eat, talk, listen to the radio, and play music. They also hang out at the *plaza*; go to *comedores*, or cafés; watch movies; or relax at nightclubs with live music and dancing.

Going to school

The school year lasts from late January to October. Children begin each day standing in *formación*, or "formation," as their teacher makes sure they are neatly dressed. Children study subjects such as language, math, geography, and science. Beginning in grade seven, they also learn English. After school, students work, play with friends, or do their homework.

There are more than 200 stores in this shopping mall in Santa Tecla, a suburb of San Salvador.

Busy markets

Most Salvadorans shop for produce or meat daily in *mercados*, or outdoor markets. Every few days, they stock up on basic foods such as corn, beans, and rice. The largest market sits in the center of town and sprawls across several streets. There, vendors set up stalls filled with all sorts of colorful goods, including fresh food, flowers, clothes, toys, books, and electronics. Women are often in charge of shopping for their family. To get through the market crowds, they sometimes carry their purchases on their heads in *canastos*, or wicker baskets.

Indoor shopping

Some Salvadorans shop for food and other necessities at their city's department stores, supermarkets, and malls, which are similar to those found in the United States and Canada. Prices are much higher than at the street markets, but there are many popular products, especially American clothing, that are hard to find elsewhere.

Sports and pastimes

After a hard day's work, Salvadorans like to have fun! They enjoy sports, games, music, dancing, and good food.

At the *plaza*

El Salvador's climate is warm, so people spend time outdoors throughout the year. The *plaza* is one of their favorite places to visit. Beautiful trees, flowers, statues, and fountains decorate the *plaza*. Some Salvadorans spend hours there, reading, taking a nap, playing sports, talking to friends, or people-watching.

On the beach

The beach is another popular place to relax, play, or have a picnic. People from all over the country pack El Salvador's lakeside and seaside beaches. Sunday afternoons, as well as holidays such as Christmas and Easter, are favorite times to go to the beach or to swim in one of the hundreds of rivers that flow through the countryside.

(top) People swim and enjoy the warm weather during their Easter vacation at Majahual Beach, on the Pacific coast.

In the game **paolo encebado**, *or "greasy wood," children try to get to the top of a slippery pole by standing on each other's shoulders. The first child to reach the top wins a small sack full of money.*

Fútbol

Fútbol, or soccer, is the most popular sport in El Salvador. Both children and adults love to play *fútbol* in parks, *plazas*, or on streets where there is little traffic. If players cannot afford a soccer ball, they sometimes make one out of a nylon stocking stuffed with rags.

Children's games

Salvadoran children love playing *mica* and *escondelero*. *Mica* is a game of tag. *Escondelero* is a combination of tag and hide-and-seek, played with a ball. To play *escondelero*, place a ball on the ground and choose one person to guard it. All the other players hide. While the guard searches for the hidden players, they try to sneak up and kick the ball. If the guard tags the other players, they are captured. If someone kicks the ball, the players are freed. The game ends when everyone is captured.

Basketball is a popular Salvadoran sport, especially in schools. Crowds of spectators often sing or play instruments to cheer on their team.

Repeat after me....

Like many other people in the world, Salvadorans speak Spanish. If you were in the *plaza* of a Salvadoran city, you might hear some of the words below:

English	Spanish
Good day, good morning	*Buenas dias*
Hello	*Hola*
Thank you	*Gracias*
You're welcome or "it was nothing"	*De nada*
Yes	*Si*
No	*No*
Kid or young boy (from the word for bug)	*Bicho*
Hey! or No way!	*Noombre!*
Holy cow!	*Puchica!*

The flavors of El Salvador

Salvadorans usually eat traditional foods made from eggs, cheese, corn, beans, squash, and rice. They also eat a lot of fruit. Meat and seafood are more expensive, so Salvadorans eat them less often. People in cities enjoy fast foods, such as hamburgers and pizzas, as well as a Salvadoran snack called a *pupusa*.

Tortillas everywhere!

Tortillas are as common in El Salvador as bread and potatoes are in North America. These round, flat cakes are made from corn. Some families take their corn to a nearby *molino*, or grinder, who crushes it into a fine flour. The family uses this flour to make *tortilla* dough. Other families make *masa*, or corn dough, by softening the kernels in water and then pounding them into a sticky mash with a grinding stone. They shape the dough into *tortillas* and cook them on a hot clay grill. When brown flecks cover the *tortillas*, they are ready to be served.

Mealtime

Salvadorans eat three main meals a day. *Desayuno*, or breakfast, is between 6:00 and 7:30 in the morning. Most people eat a *tortilla* soaked in warm milk with a cup of coffee and some fruit. *Almuerzo*, the midday meal, is often large. After a bowl of soup, people eat *tortillas* with rice, beans, corn, meat, or fish. People in the countryside might take a break, or *siesta*, after eating such a large meal. For *la cena*, or supper, people usually eat *tortillas* and vegetables. *La cena* is often late in the evening. People also eat many tropical fruits from El Salvador's Pacific shore. These include mangoes, avocados, and coconuts, as well as the sweet *nance*, a kind of red or yellow berry, and the juicy *jocote*, a fruit similar to a plum.

Pupusas

Pupusas are a Salvadoran specialty. They can be a snack or part of a larger meal. *Pupusas* are like fat *tortillas*, made of *masa* stuffed with cheese, pork, or beans. *Pupusas* are topped with *curtido*, a colorful mixture of pickled cabbage, carrots, and onions. People buy *pupusas* from streetside stands and shops called *pupuserías*. The snacks are so popular that 4:00 in the afternoon, the time that most *pupuserías* open, is known as "*pupusa* time."

*(above) A girl makes **tortillas** over a fire in her home on Monte Cristo, an island off the southern coast of El Salvador.*

*(right) A family sits down together to enjoy a meal of **tortillas, corn, meat,** and a refreshing glass of lemonade.*

Dried beans, spices, and corn are used in many Salvadoran dishes.

Fry, fry again

Salvadorans eat a lot of beans, including black beans and a red bean that is similar to a kidney bean, but smaller. They boil the dry beans until they are soft, mash them into a paste, and fry them. After a meal, they store the leftover bean paste in a clay pot. The longer it stays in the pot, the more flavorful it becomes. For the next meal, they fry the bean paste again. *Frijoles refritos*, or refried beans, mixed with vegetables, corn, and rice make a tasty meal.

Drinking beans and coconuts

The drink that El Salvador is best known for is coffee. For over a hundred years, the country has been one of the leading producers of coffee beans in the world. Hot chocolate, invented by the ancient Mayan people, is another favorite hot drink. *Horchata* is also popular. It is a sweet drink that is sometimes made of ground squash seeds, corn, and water, and sometimes made of sugar, cinnamon, and starchy water in which rice has soaked. Salvadorans also enjoy fresh fruit drinks. *Licuados* are made from fruit and milk, while *refrescos* are made from coconut and tropical fruit juices.

Bananos en gloria

Bananas are a favorite fruit in El Salvador. They are the main ingredient in this dish, called *bananos en gloria* or "glory bananas." You can serve *bananos en gloria* with refried red beans and sour cream, or eat them on their own for dessert.

It is easy to prepare *bananos en gloria* with an adult's help. You need:
a skillet
a knife
1 tablespoon (15 ml) butter or margarine
10 ripe bananas
1 tablespoon (15 ml) sugar
1 teaspoon (5 ml) cinnamon

1. Melt the butter or margarine in a hot skillet.

2. Peel and slice the bananas. Place them in the skillet.

3. Add the sugar and cinnamon.

4. Cover the skillet and lower the heat.

5. Cook for 10 to 12 minutes, until the bananas are golden brown and have a honey-like texture. This recipe serves five to ten people.

A special visit

Julia was excited. Her cousins, aunt, and uncle would be at her apartment any minute. Her father, who was tuning his guitar, spotted her waiting by the door … again. "Julia," he said, "I told you to do your geography homework until they arrive."

(top) Julia can hardly wait to get home from school to see her aunt, uncle, and cousins.

(below) Julia's uncle owns a cattle farm. Her cousins help him with the daily chores after school.

"But, Tata, I already spent the afternoon with my study group. It's the eve of Independence!" Tata turned to Mamá, who was setting the table with delicious food for their guests. Mamá said, "Oh, let her skip the books, just this once." Julia smiled at her mother, who winked back. "All right," Tata said finally, "but only if I get to eat your delicious *tortillas*."

Julia laughed as she took the grinding stones and mashed the kernels of corn. Her piping hot *tortillas* would be the finishing touch to Mamá's feast. As Julia worked over the hot griddle, she thought about their guests. "Mamá," she asked, "why did Tía Alicia and Tío José stay in the village while we moved to the city?"

"Our families have been farmers for many generations, so it's hard for José, or anybody, to leave," Mamá answered as she chopped tomatoes. "But your Tata and I heard about factory jobs in the city. We thought that coming here would mean a better life."

While shopping at the market for ingredients for dinner, Julia's mother spots fresh avocados.

Just then, Julia heard loud voices in the hall, and the door burst open. Julia's two younger brothers ran in, leading her aunt and uncle, and their four children. What a commotion! The tiny apartment was instantly packed with people. Alicia and José rushed to hug and kiss Julia, Mamá, and Tata. "Happy *Quince de Septiembre*!" each of them exclaimed.

After their greetings, José tried to find a spot for his *tambor* that was safe from all the children running around, laughing and playing. "I think my drum will be fine right here, close to these delicious-smelling *pupusas*!" he said, sitting down right in front of them.

"We had better start the meal before my brother eats all the appetizers!" Mamá joked. There was not enough room at the table for everyone to eat at the same time, so Julia's family ate in shifts. The wonderful meal included rice, squash, beans, chicken, all the *pupusas* they could eat, and for dessert, fresh fruit.

After dinner, Julia's brothers and cousins ran into the hallway for a noisy game of *mica*. Julia stayed behind to listen to the adults' conversation. "We don't have much here, but it's better than before," Tata was saying. "If you like, José, I can put in a good word for you at the factory. My godfather is a foreman there. He'll find you a job if you want one."

"We love living in the countryside," José replied, "but even though more land is being given to regular farmers like us, it's hard to make ends meet."

"If there is work and a place to live, we'll move to the city," Tía Alicia said.

"Then it's settled," Mamá said, smiling at her brother. "I can't wait to have you here to stay."

"What's all this talk about work on the eve of our holiday?" Tata cried, taking out his guitar. "Tonight we dance! And tomorrow, parades, speeches, and fireworks!" José grabbed his *tambor*. Julia smiled, happy to hear the two men play together again. As Julia's brothers and cousins came in from the hall, they joined in the singing, dancing, and laughing, until they all fell asleep, one by one.

Glossary

ancestor A person from whom one is descended

archaeologist A person who studies the past by looking at buildings and artifacts

archbishop The leader of a group of churches in a certain region

artisan A skilled craftsperson

astronomy The study of the stars and planets

capital A city where the government of a state or country is located

cathedral A large church

civil war A war between different groups of people or areas within a country

denomination A religious group within a faith

descendant A person who can trace his or her family roots to a certain family or group

fertile Able to produce abundant crops or vegetation

gourd The hard-shelled fruit of certain vines, which is dried to make musical instruments

harass To irritate or torment

humanity The human race

immigrant A person who settles in another country

independence The state of not being governed by a foreign power

indigo A plant that is used to make a blue dye

intermarry To marry someone from another culture or background

pageant A play that shows a historical event

papier-mâché Shreds of paper mixed with glue that are molded into shapes, dried, and painted

plantation A large farm on which crops, such as cotton, coffee, and sugar, are grown

ransom Payment for the release of a person

rebellion An uprising against a government

resurrection Rising from the dead or coming back to life

revolutionary A person who brings about or supports the overthrow or replacement of a government

savior A person who rescues another from harm or danger

shrine A small area or structure dedicated to a god or saint

step pyramid A four-sided structure with a rectangular base that ancient peoples used as a burial place

subject A person under the power of a leader or nation

thatch Plants, such as reeds or hay, woven together to make a roof

wicker A flexible plant branch that is woven into baskets or furniture

worship To honor or respect a god

Index

KNOPF BOOKS BY ROALD DAHL

George's Marvelous Me

ROALD DAHL

George's Marvelous Medicine

Illustrated by Quentin Blake

ALFRED A. KNOPF
New York

THIS IS A BORZOI BOOK PUBLISHED BY ALFRED A. KNOPF

Text copyright © 1981 by Roald Dahl Nominee Limited
Illustrations copyright © 1981 by Quentin Blake
Jacket illustration copyright © 1996 by Quentin Blake
All rights reserved under International and Pan-American Copyright Conventions.
Published in the United States of America by Alfred A. Knopf, a division of
Random House, Inc., New York, and simultaneously in Canada by
Random House of Canada Limited, Toronto.
Distributed by Random House, Inc., New York.
Originally published by Alfred A. Knopf, a division of Random House, Inc., in 1981.

www.randomhouse.com/kids

KNOPF, BORZOI BOOKS, and the colophon are registered trademarks of Random House, Inc.

Library of Congress Cataloging-in-Publication Data available upon request

ISBN 0-375-82206-2 (trade)
ISBN 0-375-92206-7 (lib. bdg.)

Printed in the United States of America

June 2002

10 9 8 7 6

Revised Edition

*This book is for
doctors everywhere*

CONTENTS

Grandma

"**I**'m going shopping in the village," George's mother said to George on Saturday morning. "So be a good boy and don't get into mischief."

This was a silly thing to say to a small boy at any time. It immediately made him wonder what sort of mischief he might get into.

"And don't forget to give Grandma her medicine at eleven o'clock," the mother said. Then out she went, closing the back door behind her.

Grandma, who was dozing in her chair by the window, opened one wicked little eye and said, "Now you heard what your mother said, George. Don't forget my medicine."

"No, Grandma," George said.

"And just try to behave yourself for once while she's away."

"Yes, Grandma," George said.

George was bored to tears. He didn't have a brother or a sister. His father was a farmer, and the farm they lived on was miles away from anywhere, so there were never any children to play with. He was tired of staring at pigs and hens and cows and sheep. He was especially tired of having to live in the same house as that grizzly old grunion of a grandma. Looking after her all by himself was hardly the most exciting way to spend a Saturday morning.

"You can make me a nice cup of tea for a start," Grandma said to George. "That'll keep you out of mischief for a few minutes."

"Yes, Grandma," George said.

George couldn't help disliking Grandma. She was a selfish grumpy old woman. She had pale brown teeth and a small puckered-up mouth like a dog's bottom.

"How much sugar in your tea today, Grandma?" George asked her.

"One spoonful," she said. "And no milk."

Most grandmothers are lovely, kind, helpful old ladies, but not this one. She spent all day and every day sitting in her chair by the window, and she was always complaining, grousing, grouching, grumbling, griping about something or other. Never once, even on her best days, had she smiled at George and said, "Well, how are you this morning, George?" or, "Why don't you and I have a game of Snakes and Ladders?" or, "How was school today?" She didn't seem to care about other people, only about herself. She was a miserable old grouch.

George went into the kitchen and made Grandma a cup of tea with a teabag. He put one spoon of sugar in it and no milk. He stirred the sugar well and carried the cup into the living room.

Grandma sipped the tea. "It's not sweet enough," she said. "Put more sugar in."

George took the cup back to the kitchen and added another spoonful of sugar. He stirred it again and carried it carefully in to Grandma.

2

"Where's the saucer?" she said. "I won't have a cup without a saucer."

George fetched her a saucer.

"And what about a teaspoon, if you please?"

"I've stirred it for you, Grandma. I stirred it well."

"I'll stir my own tea, thank you very much," she said. "Fetch me a teaspoon."

George fetched her a teaspoon.

When George's mother or father was home, Grandma never ordered George about like this. It was only when she had him on her own that she began treating him badly.

"You know what's the matter with you?" the old woman said, staring at George over the rim of the teacup with those bright wicked little eyes. "You're

3

growing too fast. Boys who grow too fast become stupid and lazy."

"But I can't help it if I'm growing fast, Grandma," George said.

"Of course you can," she snapped. "Growing's a nasty childish habit."

"But we *have* to grow, Grandma. If we didn't grow, we'd never be grown-ups."

"Rubbish, boy, rubbish," she said. "Look at me. Am I growing? Certainly not."

"But you did once, Grandma."

"Only *very little*," the old woman answered. "I gave up growing when I was extremely small, along with all the other nasty childish habits like laziness and disobedience and greed and sloppiness and untidiness and stupidity. You haven't given up any of these things, have you?"

"I'm still only a little boy, Grandma."

"You're eight years old," she snorted. "That's old enough to know better. If you don't stop growing soon, it'll be too late."

"Too late for what, Grandma?"

"It's ridiculous," she went on. "You're nearly as tall as me already."

George took a good look at Grandma. She certainly was a *very tiny* person. Her legs were so short she had to have a footstool to put her feet on, and her head only came halfway up the back of the armchair.

"Daddy says it's fine for a man to be tall," George said.

4

"Don't listen to your daddy," Grandma said. "Listen to me."

"But how do I stop myself growing?" George asked her.

"Eat less chocolate," Grandma said.

"Does chocolate make you grow?"

"It makes you grow the *wrong way*," she snapped. "Up instead of down."

Grandma sipped some tea but never took her eyes from the little boy who stood before her. "Never grow up," she said. "Always down."

"Yes, Grandma."

"And stop eating chocolate. Eat cabbage instead."

"Cabbage! Oh, no, I don't like cabbage," George said.

"It's not what you like or what you don't like," Grandma snapped. "It's what's good for you that counts. From now on, you must eat cabbage three times a day. Mountains of cabbage! And if it's got caterpillars in it, so much the better!"

"Ouch," George said.

"Caterpillars give you brains," the old woman said.

"Mummy washes them down the sink," George said.

"Mummy's as stupid as you are," Grandma said. "Cabbage doesn't taste of anything without a few boiled caterpillars in it. Slugs, too."

"Not *slugs!*" George cried out. "I couldn't eat slugs!"

"Whenever I see a live slug on a piece of lettuce," Grandma said, "I gobble it up quick before it crawls away. Delicious." She squeezed her lips together tight so that her mouth became a tiny wrinkled hole. "Delicious," she said again. "Worms and slugs and beetley bugs. You don't know what's good for you."

"You're joking, Grandma."

"I never joke," she said. "Beetles are perhaps best of all. They go *crunch!*"

"Grandma! That's beastly!"

The old hag grinned, showing those pale brown teeth. "Sometimes, if you're lucky," she said, "you get a beetle inside the stem of a stick of celery. That's what I like."

"Grandma! How *could* you?"

"You find all sorts of nice things in sticks of raw celery," the old woman went on. "Sometimes it's earwigs."

"I don't want to hear about it!" cried George.

"A big fat earwig is very tasty," Grandma said, licking her lips. "But you've got to be very quick, my dear, when you put one of those in your mouth. It has a pair of sharp nippers on its back end and if it grabs your tongue with those, it never lets go. So you've got to bite the earwig first, *chop chop*, before it bites you."

George started edging toward the door. He wanted to get as far away as possible from this filthy old woman.

"You're trying to get away from me, aren't you?" she said, pointing a finger straight at George's face. "You're trying to get away from Grandma."

Little George stood by the door staring at the old hag in the chair. She stared back at him.

Could it be, George wondered, that she was a witch? He had always thought witches were only in fairy tales, but now he was not so sure.

"Come closer to me, little boy," she said, beckoning to him with a horny finger. "Come closer to me and I will tell you *secrets*."

George didn't move.

Grandma didn't move either.

"I know a great many secrets," she said, and suddenly she smiled. It was a thin icy smile, the kind a snake might make just before it bites you. "Come over here to Grandma and she'll whisper secrets to you."

George took a step backward, edging closer to the door.

"You mustn't be frightened of your old grandma," she said, smiling that icy smile.

George took another step backward.

"Some of us," she said, and all at once she was leaning forward in her chair and whispering in a throaty sort of voice George had never heard her use before. "Some of us," she said, "have magic powers that can twist the creatures of this earth into wondrous shapes. . . ."

A tingle of electricity flashed down the length of George's spine. He began to feel frightened.

"Some of us," the old woman went on, "have fire on our tongues and sparks in our bellies and wizardry in the tips of our fingers. . . .

"Some of us know secrets that would make your hair stand straight up on end and your eyes pop out of their sockets. . . ."

George wanted to run away, but his feet seemed stuck to the floor.

"We know how to make your nails drop off and teeth grow out of your fingers instead."

George began to tremble. It was her face that frightened him most of all, the frosty smile, the brilliant unblinking eyes.

"We know how to have you wake up in the morning with a long tail coming out from behind you."

"Grandma!" he cried out. "Stop!"

"We know secrets, my dear, about dark places where dark things live and squirm and slither all over each other. . . ."

George made a dive for the door.

"It doesn't matter how far you run," he heard her saying, "you won't ever get away. . . ."

George ran into the kitchen, slamming the door behind him.

The Marvelous Plan

George sat himself down at the table in the kitchen. He was shaking a little. Oh, how he hated Grandma! He really *hated* that horrid old witchy woman. And all of a sudden he had a tremendous urge to *do something* about her. Something *whopping*. Something *absolutely terrific*. A *real shocker*. A sort of explosion. He wanted to blow away the witchy smell that hung about her in the next room. He may have been only eight years old, but he was a brave little boy. He was ready to take this old woman on.

"I'm not going to be frightened by *her*," he said softly to himself. But he *was* frightened. And that's why he wanted suddenly to explode her away.

Well . . . not quite away. But he did want to shake the old woman up a bit.

Very well, then. What should it be, this whopping terrific exploding shocker for Grandma?

He would have liked to put a firecracker under her chair, but he didn't have one.

He would have liked to put a long green snake down the back of her dress, but he didn't have a long green snake.

He would have liked to put six big black rats in the room with her and lock the door, but he didn't have six big black rats.

As George sat there pondering this interesting problem, his eye fell upon the bottle of Grandma's brown

medicine standing on the sideboard. Rotten stuff it seemed to be. Four times a day a large spoonful of it was shoveled into her mouth, and it didn't do her the slightest bit of good. She was always just as horrid after she'd had it as she'd been before. The whole point of medicine, surely, was to make a person better. If it didn't do that, then it was quite useless.

So-ho! thought George suddenly. *Ah-ha! Ho-hum!* I know exactly what I'll do. I shall make her a *new* medicine, one that is so strong and so fierce and so fantastic it will either cure her completely or blow off the top of her head. I'll make her a *magic medicine*, a medicine no doctor in the world has ever made before.

George looked at the kitchen clock. It said five past ten. There was nearly an hour left before Grandma's next dose was due at eleven.

"Here we go, then!" cried George, jumping up from the table. "A magic medicine it shall be!

> "So give me a bug and a jumping flea,
> Give me two snails and lizards three,
> And a slimy squiggler from the sea,
> And the poisonous sting of a bumblebee,
> And the juice from the fruit of the jujube tree,
> And the powdered bone of a wombat's knee.
> And one hundred other things as well
> Each with a rather nasty smell.
> I'll stir them up, I'll boil them long,
> A mixture tough, a mixture strong.
> And then, heigh-ho, and down it goes,

A nice big spoonful (hold your nose)
Just gulp it down and have no fear.
'How do you like it, Granny dear?'
Will she go pop? Will she explode?
Will she go flying down the road?
Will she go poof in a puff of smoke?
Start fizzing like a can of Coke?
Who knows? Not I. Let's wait and see.
(I'm glad it's neither you nor me.)
Oh Grandma, if you only knew
What I have got in store for you!"

George Begins to Make the Medicine

George took an enormous stewing pot out of the cupboard and placed it on the kitchen table.

"George!" came the shrill voice from the next room. "What are you doing?"

"Nothing, Grandma," he called out.

"You needn't think I can't hear you just because you closed the door! You're rattling the pots and pans!"

"I'm just tidying the kitchen, Grandma."

Then there was silence.

George had absolutely no doubts whatsoever about how he was going to make his famous medicine. He wasn't going to fool about wondering whether to put in a little bit of this or a little bit of that. Quite simply, he was going to put in EVERYTHING he could find. There would be no messing about, no hesitating, no wondering whether a particular thing would knock the old girl sideways or not. The rule would be this: Whatever he saw, if it was runny or powdery or gooey, in it went.

Nobody had ever made a medicine like that before. If it didn't actually cure Grandma, then it would anyway cause some exciting results. It would be worth watching.

George decided to work his way around the various rooms one at a time and see what they had to offer.

He would go first to the bathroom. There are always lots of funny things in a bathroom. So upstairs he went, carrying the enormous two-handled pot before him.

In the bathroom, he gazed longingly at the famous and dreaded medicine cupboard. But he didn't go near it. It was the only thing in the entire house he was forbidden to touch. He had made solemn promises to his parents about this, and he wasn't going to break them. There were things in there, they had told him, that could actually kill a person, and although he was out to give Grandma a pretty fiery mouthful, he didn't really want a dead body on his hands. George put the stewpot on the floor and went to work.

Number one was a bottle labeled GOLDENGLOSS HAIR SHAMPOO. He emptied it into the pot. "That ought to wash her tummy nice and clean," he said.

He took a full tube of TOOTHPASTE and squeezed out the whole lot of it in one long worm. "Maybe that will brighten up those horrid brown teeth of hers," he said.

There was an aerosol can of SUPERFOAM SHAVING SOAP belonging to his father. George loved playing with aerosols. He pressed the button and kept his finger on it until there was nothing left. A wonderful mountain of white foam built up in the giant pot.

With his fingers, he scooped out the contents of a jar of VITAMIN ENRICHED FACE CREAM.

In went a small bottle of scarlet NAIL POLISH. "If the toothpaste doesn't clean her teeth," George said, "then this will paint them as red as roses."

He found another jar of creamy stuff labeled HAIR REMOVER. SMEAR IT ON YOUR LEGS, it said, AND ALLOW TO REMAIN FOR FIVE MINUTES. George tipped it all into the pot.

There was a bottle with yellow stuff inside it called DISHWORTH'S FAMOUS DANDRUFF CURE. In it went.

There was something called BRILLIDENT FOR CLEANING FALSE TEETH. It was a white powder. In that went, too.

He found another aerosol can, NEVERMORE PONGING DEODORANT SPRAY, GUARANTEED, it said, TO KEEP AWAY UNPLEASANT BODY SMELLS FOR A WHOLE DAY. "She could use plenty of that," George said as he sprayed the entire canful into the stewing pot.

LIQUID PARAFFIN, the next one was called. It was a big bottle. He hadn't the faintest idea what it did to you, but he poured it in anyway.

That, he thought, looking around him, was about all from the bathroom.

On his mother's dressing table in the bedroom George found yet another lovely aerosol can. It was called HELGA'S HAIRSET. HOLD TWELVE INCHES AWAY FROM THE HAIR AND SPRAY LIGHTLY. He squirted the whole lot into the pot. He *did* enjoy squirting these aerosols.

There was a bottle of perfume called FLOWERS OF TURNIPS. It smelled of old cheese. In it went.

And in, too, went a large round box of POWDER that was called PINK PLASTER. There was a powder puff on top, and he threw that in as well for luck.

He found a couple of LIPSTICKS. He pulled the greasy red things out of their little cases and added them to the mixture.

The bedroom had nothing more to offer, so George carried the enormous pot downstairs again and trotted into the laundry room where the shelves were full of all kinds of household items.

The first one he took down was a large box of SUPERWHITE FOR AUTOMATIC WASHING MACHINES. DIRT, it said, WILL DISAPPEAR LIKE MAGIC. George didn't

know whether Grandma was automatic or not, but she was certainly a dirty old woman. "So she'd better have it all," he said, tipping in the whole boxful.

Then there was a big can of WAXWELL FLOOR POLISH. IT REMOVES FILTH AND FOUL MESSES FROM YOUR FLOOR AND LEAVES EVERYTHING SHINY BRIGHT, it said. George scooped the orange-colored waxy stuff out of the can and plunked it into the pot.

19

There was a round cardboard carton labeled FLEA POWDER FOR DOGS. KEEP WELL AWAY FROM THE DOG'S FOOD, it said, BECAUSE THIS POWDER, IF EATEN, WILL MAKE THE DOG EXPLODE. "Good," said George, pouring it all into the stewing pot.

He found a box of CANARY SEED on the shelf. "Perhaps it'll make the old bird sing," he said, and in it went.

Next, George explored the box with shoe-cleaning materials—brushes and cans and polishing cloths. Well now, he thought, Grandma's medicine is brown, so *my* medicine must also be brown, or she'll smell a rat. The way to color it, he decided, would be with BROWN SHOE POLISH. The large can he chose was labeled DARK TAN. Splendid. He scooped it all out with an old spoon and plopped it into the pot. He would stir it up later.

On his way back to the kitchen, George saw a bottle of GIN standing on the sideboard. Grandma was very fond of gin. She was allowed to have a small nip of it every evening. Now he would give her a treat. He would pour in the whole bottle. He did.

Back in the kitchen, George put the huge stewing pot on the table and went over to the cupboard that served as a larder. The shelves were bulging with bottles and jars of every sort. He chose the following and emptied them one by one into the pot:

A TIN OF CURRY POWDER

A TIN OF MUSTARD POWDER

A BOTTLE OF "EXTRA HOT" CHILI SAUCE

A TIN OF BLACK PEPPERCORNS

A BOTTLE OF HORSERADISH SAUCE

"There!" he said aloud. "That should do it!"

"George!" came the screechy voice from the next room. "Who are you talking to in there? What are you up to?"

"Nothing, Grandma, absolutely nothing," he called back.

"Is it time for my medicine yet?"

"No, Grandma, not for about half an hour."

"Well, just see you don't forget it."

"I won't, Grandma," George answered. "I promise I won't."

Animal Pills

At this point, George suddenly had an extra good wheeze. Although the medicine cupboard in the house was forbidden ground, what about the medicines his father kept on the shelf in the shed next to the henhouse? The animal medicines?

What about *those*?

Nobody had ever told him he mustn't touch *them*.

Let's face it, George said to himself, hair spray and shaving cream and shoe polish are all very well, and they will no doubt cause some splendid explosions inside the old geezer, but what the magic mixture now needs is a touch of the real stuff, real pills and real tonics, to give it punch and muscle.

George picked up the heavy three-quarters full pot and carried it out the back door. He crossed the farmyard and headed straight for the shed alongside the henhouse. He knew his father wouldn't be there. He was out haymaking in one of the meadows.

George entered the dusty old shed and put the stewing pot on the bench. Then he looked up at the medicine shelf. There were five big bottles there. Two were full of pills, two were full of runny stuff and one was full of powder.

"I'll use them all," George said. "Grandma needs them. Boy, does she need them!"

The first bottle he took down contained an orange-colored powder. The label said, FOR CHICKENS WITH

22

FOUL PEST, HEN GRIPE, SORE BEAKS, GAMMY LEGS, COCKERELITIS, EGG TROUBLE, BROODINESS OR LOSS OF FEATHERS. MIX ONE SPOONFUL ONLY WITH EACH BUCKET OF FEED.

"Well," George said aloud to himself as he tipped in the whole bottleful, "the old bird won't be losing any feathers after she's had a dose of this."

The next bottle he took down had about five hundred gigantic purple pills in it. FOR HORSES WITH

HOARSE THROATS, it said on the label. THE HOARSE-THROATED HORSE SHOULD SUCK ONE PILL TWICE A DAY.

"Grandma may not have a hoarse throat," George said, "but she's certainly got a sharp tongue. Maybe they'll cure that instead." Into the pot went the five hundred gigantic purple pills.

Then there was a bottle of thick yellowish liquid. FOR COWS, BULLS AND BULLOCKS, the label said. WILL CURE COWPOX, COW MANGE, CRUMPLED HORNS, BAD BREATH IN BULLS, EARACHE, TOOTHACHE, HEADACHE, HOOFACHE, TAILACHE AND SORE UDDERS.

"That grumpy old cow in the living room has every one of those rotten illnesses," George said. "She'll need it all." With a slop and a gurgle, the yellow liquid splashed into the now nearly full stewpot.

The next bottle contained a brilliant red liquid. SHEEPDIP, it said on the label. FOR SHEEP WITH SHEEP ROT AND FOR GETTING RID OF TICKS AND FLEAS. MIX ONE SPOONFUL IN ONE GALLON OF WATER AND SLOSH IT OVER

THE SHEEP. CAUTION, DO NOT MAKE THE MIXTURE ANY STRONGER OR THE WOOL WILL FALL OUT AND THE ANIMAL WILL BE NAKED.

"By gum," said George, "how I'd love to walk in and slosh it all over old Grandma and watch the ticks and fleas go jumping off her. But I can't. I mustn't. So she'll have to drink it instead." He poured the bright red medicine into the pot.

The last bottle on the shelf was full of pale green pills. PIG PILLS, the label announced. FOR PIGS WITH PORK PRICKLES, TENDER TROTTERS, BRISTLE BLIGHT AND SWINE SICKNESS. GIVE ONE PILL PER DAY. IN SEVERE CASES TWO PILLS MAY BE GIVEN, BUT MORE THAN THAT WILL MAKE THE PIG ROCK AND ROLL.

"Just the stuff," said George, "for that miserable old pig back there in the house. She'll need a very big dose." He tipped all the green pills, hundreds and hundreds of them, into the stewing pot.

There was an old stick lying on the bench that had been used for stirring paint. George picked it up and started to stir his marvelous concoction. The mixture was as thick as cream, and as he stirred and stirred, many wonderful colors rose up from the depths and blended together, pinks, blues, greens, yellows and browns.

George went on stirring until it was all well mixed, but even so there were still hundreds of pills lying on the bottom that hadn't melted. And there was his mother's splendid powder puff floating on the surface. "I shall have to boil it all," George said. "One good quick boil on the stove is all it needs." And with that

25

he staggered back toward the house with the enormous heavy stewing pot.

On the way, he passed the garage, so he went in to see if he could find any other interesting things. He added the following:

Half a pint of ENGINE OIL—to keep Grandma's engine going smoothly.

Some ANTIFREEZE—to keep her radiator from freezing up in winter.

A handful of GREASE—to grease her creaking joints.

Then back to the kitchen.

The Cook-up

In the kitchen, George put the heavy stewing pot on the stove and turned up the gas flame underneath it as high as it would go.

"George!" came the awful voice from the next room. "It's time for my medicine!"

"Not yet, Grandma," George called back. "There's still twenty minutes before eleven o'clock."

"What mischief are you up to in there now?" Granny screeched. "I hear noises."

George thought it best not to answer this one. He found a long wooden spoon in a kitchen drawer and began stirring hard. The stuff in the pot got hotter and hotter.

Soon the marvelous mixture began to froth and foam. A rich blue smoke, the color of peacocks, rose from the surface of the liquid, and a fiery fearsome smell filled the kitchen. It made George choke and splutter. It was a smell unlike any he had smelled before. It was a brutal and bewitching smell, spicy and staggering, fierce and frenzied, full of wizardry and

magic. Whenever he got a whiff of it up his nose, fire-crackers went off in his skull and electric prickles ran along the backs of his legs. It was wonderful to stand there stirring this amazing mixture and to watch it smoking blue and bubbling and frothing and foaming as though it were alive. At one point, he could have sworn he saw bright sparks flashing in the swirling foam.

And suddenly George found himself dancing around the steaming pot, chanting strange words that came into his head out of nowhere:

> "Fiery broth and witch's brew
> Foamy froth and riches blue
> Fume and spume and spoondrift spray
> Fizzle swizzle shout hooray
> Watch it sloshing, swashing, sploshing
> Hear it hissing, squishing, spissing
> Grandma better start to pray."

Brown Paint

George turned off the heat under the stewing pot. He must leave plenty of time for it to cool down.

When all the steam and froth had gone away, he peered into the giant pot to see what color the great medicine now was. It was a deep and brilliant blue.

"It needs more brown in it," George said. "It simply must be brown, or she'll get suspicious."

George ran outside and dashed into his father's toolshed where all the paints were kept. There was a row of cans on the shelf, all colors, black, green, red, pink, white and brown. He reached for the can of brown. The label said simply DARK BROWN GLOSS PAINT ONE QUART. He took a screwdriver and prised off the lid. The can was three-quarters full. He rushed it back to the kitchen. He poured the whole lot into the pot. The pot was now full to the brim. Very gently, George stirred the paint into the mixture with the long wooden spoon. *Ah-ha!* It was all turning brown! A lovely rich creamy brown!

"Where's that medicine of mine, boy?!" came the voice from the living room. "You're forgetting me! You're doing it on purpose! I shall tell your mother!"

"I'm not forgetting you, Grandma," George called back. "I'm thinking of you all the time. But there are still ten minutes to go."

"You're a nasty little maggot!" The voice screeched

back. "You're a lazy and disobedient little worm and you're growing too fast."

George fetched the bottle of Grandma's real medicine from the sideboard. He took out the cork and tipped it all down the sink. He then filled the bottle with his own magic mixture by dipping a small jug into the pot and using it as a pourer. He replaced the cork.

Had it cooled down enough yet? Not quite. He held the bottle under the cold tap for a couple of minutes. The label came off in the water, but that didn't matter. He dried the bottle with a dishcloth.

All was now ready!

This was it!

The great moment had arrived!

"Medicine time, Grandma!" he called out.

"I should hope so, too," came the grumpy reply.

The silver tablespoon in which the medicine was always given lay ready on the kitchen sideboard. George picked it up.

Holding the spoon in one hand and the bottle in the other, he advanced into the living room.

Grandma Gets the Medicine

Grandma sat hunched in her chair by the window. The wicked little eyes followed George closely as he crossed the room toward her.

"You're late," she snapped.

"I don't think I am, Grandma."

"Don't interrupt me in the middle of a sentence!" she shouted.

"But you'd finished your sentence, Grandma."

"There you go again!" she cried. "Always interrupting and arguing. You really are a tiresome little boy. What's the time?"

"It's exactly eleven o'clock, Grandma."

"You're lying as usual. Stop talking so much and give me my medicine. Shake the bottle first. Then pour it onto the spoon and make sure it's a whole spoonful."

"Are you going to gulp it all down in one go?" George asked her. "Or will you sip it?"

"What I do is none of your business," the old woman said. "Fill the spoon."

As George removed the cork and began very slowly to pour the thick brown stuff into the spoon, he couldn't help thinking back on all the mad and marvelous things that had gone into the making of this crazy stuff—the shaving soap, the hair remover, the dandruff cure, the automatic washing-machine powder, the flea powder for dogs, the shoe polish, the black pepper, the horseradish sauce and all the rest of them,

31

not to mention the powerful animal pills and powders and liquids . . . and the brown paint.

"Open your mouth wide, Grandma," he said, "and I'll pop it in."

The old hag opened her small wrinkled mouth, showing disgusting pale brown teeth.

"Here we go!" George cried out. "Swallow it down!" He pushed the spoon well into her mouth and tipped the mixture down her throat. Then he stepped back to watch the result.

It was worth watching.

Grandma yelled *"Oweeeee!"* and her whole body shot up *whoosh* into the air. It was exactly as though someone had pushed an electric wire through the underneath of her chair and switched on the current. Up she went like a jack-in-the-box . . . and she didn't come down . . . she stayed there . . . suspended in midair . . . about two feet up . . . still in a sitting position . . . but rigid now . . . frozen . . . quivering . . . the eyes bulging . . . the hair standing straight up on end.

"Is something wrong, Grandma?" George asked her politely. "Are you all right?"

Suspended up there in space, the old girl was beyond speaking.

The shock that George's marvelous mixture had given her must have been tremendous.

You'd have thought she'd swallowed a red-hot poker the way she took off from that chair.

Then down she came again with a *plop*, back into her seat.

"Call the fire department!" she shouted suddenly. "My stomach's on fire!"

"It's just the medicine, Grandma," George said. "It's good strong stuff."

"Fire!" the old woman yelled. "Fire in the basement! Get a bucket! Man the hoses! Do something quick!"

"Cool it, Grandma," George said. But he got a bit of a shock when he saw the smoke coming out of her mouth and out of her nostrils. Clouds of black smoke were coming out of her nose and blowing around the room.

"By golly, you really are on fire," George said.

"Of course I'm on fire!" she yelled. "I'll be burned to a crisp! I'll be fried to a frizzle! I'll be boiled like a beetroot!"

George ran into the kitchen and came back with a jug of water. "Open your mouth, Grandma!" he cried. He could hardly see her for the smoke, but he managed to pour half a jugful down her throat. A sizzling sound, the kind you get if you hold a hot frying pan under cold water, came up from deep down in Grandma's stomach. The old hag bucked and shied and snorted. She gasped and gurgled. Spouts of water came shooting out of her. And the smoke cleared away.

"The fire's out," George announced proudly. "You'll be all right now, Grandma."

"*All right?*" she yelled. "Who's *all right?* There's jacky-jumpers in my tummy! There's squigglers in my belly! There's bangers in my bottom!" She began bouncing up and down in the chair. Quite obviously, she was not very comfortable.

"You'll find it's doing you a lot of good, that medicine, Grandma," George said.

"*Good?*" she screamed. "Doing me *good?* It's *killing* me!"

Then she began to bulge.

She was swelling.

She was puffing up all over!

Someone was pumping her up, that's how it looked!

Was she going to explode?

Her face was turning from purple to green!

But wait! She had a puncture somewhere! George could hear the hiss of escaping air. She stopped swelling. She was going down. She was slowly getting thinner again, shrinking back and back slowly to her shrivelly old self.

"How's things, Grandma?" George said.

No answer.

Then a funny thing happened. Grandma's body gave a sudden sharp twist and a sudden sharp jerk and she flipped herself clear out of the chair and landed neatly on her two feet on the carpet.

"That's terrific, Grandma!" George cried. "You haven't stood up like that for years! Look at you! You're standing up all on your own and you're not even using a stick!"

Grandma didn't even hear him. The frozen pop-

eyed look was back with her again now. She was miles away in another world.

Marvelous medicine, George told himself. He found it fascinating to stand there watching what it was doing to the old hag. What next? he wondered.

He soon found out.

Suddenly she began to grow.

It was quite slow at first . . . just a very gradual inching upward . . . up, up, up . . . inch by inch . . . getting taller and taller . . . about an inch every few seconds . . . and in the beginning George didn't notice it.

But when she had passed the five-foot-six mark and was going on up toward being six feet tall, George gave a jump and shouted, "Hey, Grandma! You're *growing!* You're *going up!* Hang on, Grandma! You'd better stop now or you'll be hitting the ceiling!"

But Grandma didn't stop.

It was a truly fantastic sight, this ancient scrawny old woman getting taller and taller, longer and longer, thinner and thinner, as though she were a piece of elastic being pulled upward by invisible hands.

When the top of her head actually touched the ceiling, George thought she was bound to stop.

But she didn't.

There was a sort of scrunching noise, and bits of plaster and cement came raining down.

"Hadn't you better stop now, Grandma?" George said. "Daddy's just had this whole room repainted."

37

But there was no stopping her now.

Soon, her head and shoulders had completely disappeared through the ceiling, and she was still going.

George dashed upstairs to his own bedroom, and there she was, coming up through the floor like a mushroom.

"Whoopee!" she shouted, finding her voice at last. "Hallelujah, here I come!"

"Steady, Grandma," George said.

"With a heigh-nonny-no and up we go!" she shouted. "Just watch me grow!"

"This is *my* room," George said. "Look at the mess you're making."

"Terrific medicine!" she cried. "Give me some more!"

She's dotty as a doughnut, George thought.

"Come on, boy! Give me some more!" she yelled. "Dish it out! I'm slowing down!"

George was still clutching the medicine bottle in one

hand and the spoon in the other. Oh well, he thought, why not? He poured out a second dose and popped it into her mouth.

"*Oweee!*" she screamed, and up she went again. Her feet were still on the floor downstairs in the living room, but her head was moving quickly toward the ceiling of the bedroom.

"I'm on my way now, boy!" she called down to George. "Just watch me go!"

"That's the attic above you, Grandma!" George called out. "I'd keep out of there! It's full of bugs and bogles!"

Crash! The old girl's head went through the ceiling as though it were butter.

George stood in his bedroom gazing at the shambles. There was a big hole in the floor and another in the ceiling, and sticking up like a post between the two was the middle part of Grandma. Her legs were in the room below, her head in the attic.

"I'm still going!" came the old screechy voice from up above. "Give me another dose, my boy, and let's go through the roof!"

"No, Grandma, no!" George called back. "You're busting up the whole house!"

"To heck with the house!" she shouted. "I want some fresh air! I haven't been outside for twenty years!"

"By golly, she *is* going through the roof!" George told himself. He ran downstairs. He rushed out the back door into the yard. It would be simply awful, he thought, if she bashed up the roof as well. His father would be furious. And he, George, would get the blame. *He* had made the medicine. *He* had given her too much. "Don't come through the roof, Grandma," he prayed. "Please don't."

The Brown Hen

George stood in the farmyard looking up at the roof. The old farmhouse had a fine roof of pale red tiles and tall chimneys.

There was no sign of Grandma. There was only a song thrush sitting on one of the chimney pots, singing a song. The old wurzel's got stuck in the attic, George thought. Thank goodness for that.

Suddenly a tile came clattering down from the roof and fell into the yard. The thrush took off fast and flew away.

Then another tile came down.

Then half a dozen more.

And then, very slowly, like some weird monster rising up from the deep, Grandma's head came through the roof. . . .

Then her scrawny neck. . . .

And the tops of her shoulders. . . .

"How'm I doing, boy!" she shouted. "How's that for a bash up?"

"Don't you think you'd better stop now, Grandma?" George called out.

"I have stopped!" she answered. "I feel terrific! Didn't I tell you I had magic powers! Didn't I warn you I had wizardry in the tips of my fingers! But you wouldn't listen to me, would you? You wouldn't listen to your old Grandma!"

"*You* didn't do it, Grandma," George shouted back

to her. "*I* did it! I made you a new medicine!"

"A *new medicine? You?* What rubbish!" she yelled.

"I did! I did!" George shouted.

"You're lying as usual!" Grandma yelled. "You're always lying!"

"I'm not lying, Grandma. I swear I'm not."

The wrinkled old face high up on the roof stared down suspiciously at George. "Are you telling me you actually made a new medicine all by yourself?" she shouted.

"Yes, Grandma, all by myself."

"I don't believe you," she answered. "But I'm very comfortable up here. Fetch me a cup of tea."

A brown hen was pecking about in the yard close to where George was standing. The hen gave him an idea. Quickly, he uncorked the medicine bottle and poured some of the brown stuff into the spoon. "Watch this, Grandma!" he shouted. He crouched down, holding out the spoon to the hen.

"Chicken," he said. "Chick-chick-chicken. Come here. Have some of this."

Chickens are stupid birds, and very greedy. They think everything is food. This one thought the spoon was full of corn. It hopped over. It put its head on one side and looked at the spoon. "Come on, chicken," George said. "Good chicken. Chick-chick-chick."

The brown hen stretched out its neck toward the spoon and went *peck*. It got a beakful of medicine.

The effect was electric.

"*Oweee!*" shrieked the hen and it shot straight up into the air like a rocket. It went as high as the house.

Then down it came again into the yard, *splosh*. And there it sat with its feathers all sticking straight out from its body. There was a look of amazement on its silly face. George stood watching it. Grandma up on the roof was watching it, too.

The hen got to its feet. It was rather shaky. It was making funny gurgling noises in its throat. Its beak was opening and shutting. It seemed like a pretty sick hen.

"You've done it in, you stupid boy!" Grandma shouted. "That hen's going to die! Your father'll be after you now! He'll give you socks and serve you right!"

All of a sudden, black smoke started pouring out of the hen's beak.

"It's on fire!" Grandma yelled. "The hen's on fire!"

George ran to the water trough to get a bucket of water.

"That hen'll be roasted and ready for eating any moment!" Grandma shouted.

George sloshed the bucket of water over the hen. There was a sizzling sound, and the smoke went away.

"Old hen's laid its last egg!" Grandma shouted. "Hens don't do any laying after they've been on fire!"

Now that the fire was out, the hen seemed better. It stood up properly. It flapped its wings. Then it crouched down low to the ground, as though getting ready to jump. It did jump. It jumped high in the air and turned a complete somersault, then landed back on its feet.

"It's a circus hen!" Grandma shouted from the rooftop. "It's a flipping acrobat!"

Now the hen began to grow.

45

George had been waiting for this to happen. "It's growing!" he yelled. "It's growing, Grandma! Look, it's growing!"

Bigger and bigger . . . taller and taller it grew. Soon the hen was four or five times its normal size.

"Can you see it, Grandma?" George shouted.

"I can see it, boy!" the old woman shouted back. "I'm watching it!"

George was hopping about from one foot to the other with excitement, pointing at the enormous hen and shouting, "It's had the magic medicine, Grandma, and it's growing just like you did!"

But there was a difference between the way the hen was growing and the way Grandma grew. When Grandma grew taller and taller, she got thinner and thinner. The hen didn't. It stayed nice and plump all along.

Soon it was taller than George, but it didn't stop there. It went right on growing until it was about as big as a horse. Then it stopped.

"Doesn't it look marvelous, Grandma!" George shouted.

"It's not as tall as me!" Grandma sang out. "Compared with me, that hen is titchy small! I am the tallest of them all!"

The Pig, the Bullocks, the Sheep, the Pony and the Nanny Goat

At that moment, George's mother came back from shopping in the village. She drove her car into the yard and got out. She was carrying a bottle of milk in one hand and a bag of groceries in the other.

The first thing she saw was the gigantic brown hen towering over little George. She dropped the bottle of milk.

Then Grandma started shouting at her from the rooftop, and when she looked up and saw Grandma's head sticking up through the tiles, she dropped the bag of groceries.

"How about that then, eh, Mary?" Grandma shouted. "I'll bet you've never seen a hen as big as that! That's George's giant hen, that is!"

"But . . . but . . . but . . . ." stammered George's mother.

"It's George's magic medicine!" Grandma shouted. "We've both of us had it, the hen and I!"

"But how in the world did you get up on the roof?" cried the mother.

"I didn't!" cackled the old woman. "My feet are still standing on the floor in the living room!"

This was too much for George's mother to understand. She just goggled and gaped. She looked as though she was going to faint.

A second later, George's father appeared. His name was Mr. Killy Kranky. Mr. Kranky was a small man

with bandy legs and a huge head. He was a kind father
to George, but he was not an easy person to live with
because even the smallest things got him all worked up
and excited. The hen standing in the yard was certainly not a small thing, and when Mr. Kranky saw it, he
started jumping about as though something was burn-
ing his feet. "Great heavens!" he cried, waving his
arms. "What's this? What's happened? Where did it
come from? It's a giant hen! Who did it?"

"I did," George said.

"Look at *me*!" Grandma shouted from the rooftop.
"Never mind about the hen! What about *me*?"

Mr. Kranky looked up and saw Grandma. "Shut up, Grandma," he said. It didn't seem to surprise him that the old girl was sticking up through the roof. It was the hen that excited him. He had never seen anything like it. But then who had?

"It's fantastic!" Mr. Kranky shouted, dancing around and around. "It's colossal! It's gigantic! It's tremendous! It's a miracle! How did you do it, George?"

George started telling his father about the magic medicine. While he was doing this, the big brown hen sat down in the middle of the yard and went *cluck-cluck-cluck* . . . *cluck-cluck-cluck-cluck-cluck*.

Everyone stared at it.

When it stood up again, there was a brown egg lying there. The egg was the size of a football.

"That egg would make scrambled eggs for twenty people!" Mrs. Kranky said.

"George!" Mr. Kranky shouted. "How much of this medicine have you got?"

"Lots," George said. "There's a big potful in the kitchen, and this bottle here's nearly full."

"Come with me!" Mr. Kranky yelled, grabbing George by the arm. "Bring the medicine! For years and years I've been trying to breed bigger and bigger animals. Bigger bulls for beef. Bigger pigs for pork. Bigger sheep for mutton. . . ."

They went to the pigsty first.

George gave a spoonful of the medicine to the pig.

The pig blew smoke from its nose and jumped about all over the place. Then it grew and grew.

In the end, it looked like this. . . .

They went to the herd of fine black bullocks that
Mr. Kranky was trying to fatten for the market.

George gave each of them some medicine, and this is
what happened. . . .

53

Then the sheep. . . .

He gave some to his gray pony, Jack Frost. . . .

And finally, just for fun, he gave some to Alma, the nanny goat. . . .

A Crane for Grandma

Grandma, from high up on the rooftop, could see everything that was going on, and she didn't like what she saw. She wanted to be the center of attention, and nobody was taking the slightest notice of her. George and Mr. Kranky were running around and getting excited about the enormous animals. Mrs. Kranky was washing up in the kitchen, and Grandma was all alone on the rooftop.

"Hey you!" she yelled. "George! Get me a cup of tea this minute, you idle little beast!"

"Don't listen to the old goat," Mr. Kranky said. "She's stuck where she is, and a good thing, too."

"But we can't leave her up there, Dad," George said. "What if it rains?"

"George!" Grandma yelled. "Oh, you horrible little boy! You disgusting little worm! Fetch me a cup of tea at once and a slice of currant cake!"

"We'll have to get her out, Dad," George said. "She won't give us any peace if we don't."

Mrs. Kranky came outside, and she agreed with George. "She's my own mother," she said.

"She's a pain in the neck," Mr. Kranky said.

"I don't care," Mrs. Kranky said. "I'm not leaving my own mother sticking up through the roof for the rest of her life."

So in the end, Mr. Kranky telephoned the Crane Company and asked them to send their biggest crane out to the house at once.

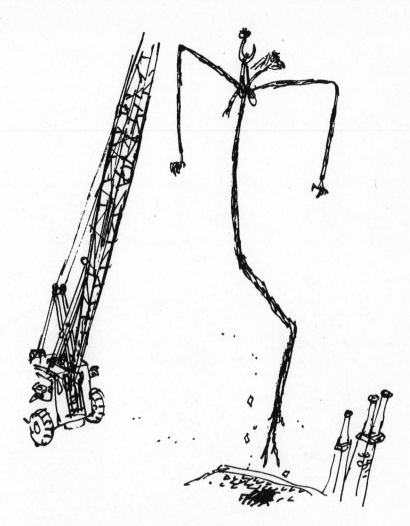

The crane arrived one hour later. It was on wheels, and there were two men inside it. The crane men climbed up onto the roof and put ropes under Grandma's arms. Then she was lifted right up through the roof. . . .

In a way, the medicine had done Grandma good. It had not made her any less grumpy or bad-tempered,

but it seemed to have cured all her aches and pains,
and she was suddenly as frisky as a ferret. As soon as
the crane had lowered her to the ground, she ran over
to George's huge pony, Jack Frost, and jumped onto
his back. This ancient old hag, who was now as tall as a

house, then galloped about the farm on the gigantic
pony, jumping over trees and sheds and shouting,
"Out of my way! Clear the decks! Stand back all you
miserable midgets or I'll trample you to death!" and
other silly things like that.

But because Grandma was now much too tall to get back into the house, she had to sleep that night in the hay barn with the mice and the rats.

Mr. Kranky's Great Idea

The next day, George's father came down to breakfast in a state of greater excitement than ever. "I've been awake all night thinking about it!" he cried.

"About what, Dad?" George asked him.

"About your marvelous medicine, of course! We can't stop now, my boy! We must start making more of it at once! More and more and more!"

The giant stewing pot had been completely emptied the day before because there had been so many sheep and pigs and cows and bullocks to be dosed.

"But why do we need more, Dad?" George asked. "We've done all our own animals, and we've made Grandma feel as frisky as a ferret, even though she does have to sleep in the barn."

"My dear boy," cried Mr. Killy Kranky, "we need barrels and barrels of it! Tons and tons! Then we will sell it to every farmer in the world so that all of them can have giant animals! We will build a Marvelous Medicine Factory and sell the stuff in bottles at ten dollars apiece. We will become rich, and you will become famous!"

"But wait a minute, Dad," George said.

"There's no waiting!" cried Mr. Kranky, working himself up so much that he put butter in his coffee and milk on his toast. "Don't you understand what this tremendous invention of yours is going to do to the world? Nobody will ever go hungry again!"

"Why won't they?" asked George.

"Because one giant cow will give fifty buckets of milk a day!" cried Mr. Kranky, waving his arms. "One giant chicken will make a hundred fried chicken dinners, and one giant pig will give you a thousand pork chops! It's tremendous, my dear boy! It's fantastic! It'll change the world."

"But wait a minute, Dad," George said again.

"Don't keep saying wait a minute!" shouted Mr. Kranky. "There isn't a minute to *wait!* We must get cracking at once!"

"Do calm down, my dear," Mrs. Kranky said from the other end of the table. "And stop putting marmalade on your cornflakes."

"The heck with my cornflakes!" cried Mr. Kranky, leaping up from his chair. "Come on, George! Let's get going! And the first thing we'll do is to make one more stewpotful as a tester."

"But, Dad," said little George. "The trouble is . . ."

"There won't be any trouble, my boy!" cried Mr. Kranky. "How can there possibly be any trouble? All you've got to do is put the same stuff into the pot as you did yesterday. And while you're doing it, I'll write down each and every item. That's how we'll get the magic recipe!"

"But, Dad," George said. "Please listen to me."

"Why don't you listen to him?" Mrs. Kranky said. "The boy's trying to tell you something."

But Mr. Kranky was too excited to listen to anyone except himself. "And then," he cried, "when the new mixture is ready, we'll test it out on an old hen just to make sure we've got it right, and after that we'll all shout hooray and build the giant factory!"

"But, Dad . . ."

"Come on then, what is it you want to say?"

"I can't possibly remember all the hundreds of things I put into the pot to make the medicine," George said.

"Of course you can, my dear boy," cried Mr. Kranky. "I'll help you! I'll jog your memory! You'll get it in the end, you see if you don't! Now then, what was the very first thing you put in?"

"I went up to the bathroom first," George said. "I used a lot of things in the bathroom and on mummy's dressing table."

"Come on, then!" cried Mr. Kranky. "Up we go to the bathroom!"

When they got there, they found, of course, a whole lot of empty tubes and empty aerosol cans and empty

bottles. "That's great," said Mr. Kranky. "That tells us exactly what you used. If anything is empty, it means you used it."

So Mr. Kranky started making a list of everything that was empty in the bathroom. Then they went to Mrs. Kranky's dressing table. "A box of powder," said Mr. Kranky, writing it down. "Helga's Hair Set. Flowers of Turnips perfume. Terrific. This is going to be easy. Where did you go next?"

"To the laundry room," George said. "But are you sure you haven't missed anything up here, Dad?"

"That's up to you, my boy," Mr. Kranky said. "Have I?"

"I don't think so," George said. So down they went to the laundry room, and once again Mr. Kranky wrote down the names of all the empty bottles and cans. "My goodness me, what a mass of stuff you used!" he cried. "No wonder it did magic things! Is that the lot?"

"No, Dad, it's not," George said, and he led his father out to the shed where the animal medicines were kept and showed him the five big empty bottles up on the shelf. Mr. Kranky wrote down all their names.

"Anything else?" Mr. Kranky asked.

Little George scratched his head and thought and thought, but he couldn't remember having put anything else in.

Mr. Killy Kranky leapt into his car and drove down to the village and bought new bottles and tubes and cans of everything on his list. He then went to the vet and got a fresh supply of all the animal medicines George had used.

"Now show me how you did it, George," he said. "Come along. Show me exactly how you mixed them all together."

Marvelous Medicine Number Two

They were in the kitchen now and the big stewing pot was on the stove. All the things Mr. Kranky had bought were lined up near the sink.

"Come along, my boy!" cried Mr. Killy Kranky. "Which one did you put in first?"

"This one," George said. "Goldengloss Hair Shampoo." He emptied the bottle into the pot.

"Now the toothpaste," George went on. . . . "And the shaving soap . . . and the face cream . . . and the nail polish . . ."

"Keep at it, my boy!" cried Mr. Kranky, dancing around the kitchen. "Keep putting them in! Don't stop! Don't pause! Don't hesitate! It's a pleasure, my dear fellow, to watch you work!"

One by one, George poured and squeezed the things into the stewing pot. With everything so close at hand, the whole job didn't take him more than ten minutes. But when it was all done, the pot didn't somehow seem to be quite as full as it had been the first time.

"*Now* what did you do?" cried Mr. Kranky. "Did you stir it?"

"I boiled it," George said. "But not for long. And I stirred it as well."

So Mr. Kranky lit the gas under the pot and George stirred the mixture with the same long wooden spoon he had used before. "It's not brown enough," George said. "Wait a minute! I know what I've forgotten!"

"What?" cried Mr. Kranky. "Tell me, quick! Because if we've forgotten even one tiny thing, then it won't work! At least not in the same way."

"A quart of brown gloss paint," George said. "That's what I've forgotten."

Mr. Killy Kranky shot out of the house and into his car like a rocket. He sped down to the village and bought the paint and rushed back again. He opened the can in the kitchen and handed it to George. George poured the paint into the stewing pot.

"Ah-ha! That's better," George said. "That's more like the right color."

"It's boiling!" cried Mr. Kranky. "It's boiling and bubbling, George! Is it ready yet?"

"It's ready," George said. "At least I hope it is."

"Right!" shouted Mr. Kranky, hopping about. "Let's test it! Let's give some to a chicken!"

"My heavens alive, why don't you calm down a bit?" Mrs. Kranky said, coming into the kitchen.

"*Calm down?*" cried Mr. Kranky. "You expect me to *calm down* and here we are mixing up the greatest medicine ever discovered in the history of the world! Come along, George! Dip a cupful out of the pot and get a spoon and we'll give some to a chicken just to make absolutely certain we've got the correct mixture."

Outside in the yard, there were several chickens that hadn't had any of George's Marvelous Medicine Number One. They were pecking about in the dirt in that silly way chickens do.

George crouched down, holding out a spoonful of Marvelous Medicine Number Two. "Come on, chick-

en," he said. "Good chicken. Chick-chick-chick."

A white chicken with black specks on its feathers looked up at George. It walked over to the spoon and went *peck*.

The effect that Medicine Number Two had on this chicken was not quite the same as the effect produced by Medicine Number One, but it was very interesting. "*Whooosh!*" shrieked the chicken and it shot six feet up in the air and came down again. Then *sparks* came flying out of its beak, bright yellow sparks of fire, as though someone was sharpening a knife on a grindstone inside its tummy. Then its legs began to grow longer. Its body stayed the same size, but the two thin yellow legs got longer and longer and longer . . . and longer still. . . .

"What's happening to it?" cried Mr. Killy Kranky.

"Something's wrong," George said.

The legs went on growing and the more they grew, the higher up into the air went the chicken's body. When the legs were about fifteen feet long, they stopped growing. The chicken looked perfectly absurd with its long long legs and its ordinary little body perched high up on top. It was like a chicken on stilts.

"Oh my sainted aunts!" cried Mr. Killy Kranky. "We've got it wrong! This chicken's no good to anybody! It's all legs! No one wants chicken legs!"

"I must have left something out," George said.

"I *know* you left something out!" cried Mr. Kranky. "Think, boy, think! What was it you left out?"

"I've got it!" said George.

"What was it, quick?"

"Flea powder for dogs," George said.

"You mean you put *flea* powder in the first one?"

"Yes, Dad, I did. A whole carton of it."

"Then that's the answer!"

"Wait a minute," said George. "Did we have brown shoe polish on our list?"

"We did not," said Mr. Kranky.

"I used that, too," said George.

"Well, no *wonder* it went wrong," said Mr. Kranky. He was already running to his car, and soon he was heading down to the village to buy more flea powder and more shoe polish.

Marvelous Medicine Number Three

"Here it is!" cried Mr. Killy Kranky, rushing into the kitchen. "One carton of flea powder for dogs and one can of brown shoe polish!"

George poured the flea powder into the giant stewing pot. Then he scooped the shoe polish out of its can and added that as well.

"Stir it up, George!" shouted Mr. Kranky. "Give it another boil! We've got it this time! I'll bet we've got it!"

After Marvelous Medicine Number Three had been boiled and stirred, George took a cupful of it out into the yard to try it on another chicken. Mr. Kranky ran after him, flapping his arms and hopping with excitement. "Come and watch this one!" he called out to Mrs. Kranky. "Come and watch us turning an ordinary chicken into a lovely great big one that lays eggs as large as footballs!"

"I hope you do better than last time," said Mrs. Kranky, following them out.

"Come on, chicken," said George, holding out a spoonful of Medicine Number Three. "Good chicken. Chick-chick-chick-chick-chick. Have some of this lovely medicine."

A magnificent black cockerel with a scarlet comb came stepping over. The cockerel looked at the spoon and it went *peck*.

"*Cock-a-doodle-do!*" squawked the cockerel, shooting up into the air and coming down again.

73

"Watch him now!" cried Mr. Kranky. "Watch him grow! Any moment he's going to start getting bigger and bigger!"

Mr. Killy Kranky, Mrs. Kranky and little George stood in the yard staring at the black cockerel. The cockerel stood quite still. It looked as though it had a headache.

"What's happening to its neck?" Mrs. Kranky said.

"It's getting longer," George said.

"I'll say it's getting longer," Mrs. Kranky said.

Mr. Kranky, for once, said nothing.

"Last time it was the legs," Mrs. Kranky said. "Now it's the neck. Who wants a chicken with a long neck? You can't eat a chicken's neck."

It was an extraordinary sight. The cockerel's body hadn't grown at all. But the neck was now about six feet long.

"All right, George," Mr. Kranky said. "What else have you forgotten?"

74

"I don't know," George said.

"Oh, yes you do," Mr. Kranky said. "Come on, boy, *think*. There's probably just one vital thing missing, and you've got to remember it."

"I put in some engine oil from the garage," George said. "Did you have that on your list?"

"Eureka!" cried Mr. Kranky. "That's the answer! How much did you put in?"

"Half a pint," George said.

Mr. Kranky ran to the garage and found another half pint of oil. "And some antifreeze," George called after him. "I sloshed in a bit of antifreeze."

Marvelous Medicine Number Four

Back in the kitchen once again, George, with Mr. Kranky watching him anxiously, tipped half a pint of engine oil and some antifreeze into the giant stewing pot.

"Boil it up again!" cried Mr. Kranky. "Boil it and stir it!"

George boiled it and stirred it.

"You'll never get it right," said Mrs. Kranky. "Don't forget you don't just have to have the same things but you've got to have exactly the same *amounts* of those things. And how can you possibly do that?"

"You keep out of this!" cried Mr. Kranky. "We're doing fine! We've got it this time, you see if we haven't!"

This was George's Marvelous Medicine Number Four, and when it had boiled for a couple of minutes, George once again carried a cupful of it out into the yard. Mr. Kranky ran after him. Mrs. Kranky followed more slowly. "You're going to have some mighty queer chickens around here if you go on like this," she said.

"Dish it out, George!" cried Mr. Kranky. "Give a spoonful to that one over there!" He pointed to a brown hen.

George knelt down and held out the spoon with the new medicine in it. "Chick-chick," he said. "Try some of this."

The brown hen walked over and looked at the spoon. Then it went *peck*.

"*Ouch!*" it said. Then a funny whistling noise came out of its beak.

"Watch it grow!" shouted Mr. Kranky.

"Don't be too sure," said Mrs. Kranky. "Why is it whistling like that?"

"Keep quiet, woman!" cried Mr. Kranky. "Give it a chance!"

They stood there staring at the brown hen.

"It's getting smaller," George said. "Look at it, Dad. It's shrinking."

And indeed it was. In less than a minute, the hen had shrunk so much it was no bigger than a new-hatched chick. It looked ridiculous.

Goodbye, Grandma

"There's still something you've left out," Mr. Kranky said.

"I can't think what it could be," George said.

"Give it up," Mrs. Kranky said. "Pack it in. You'll never get it right."

Mr. Kranky looked very forlorn.

George looked pretty fed up, too. He was still kneeling on the ground with the spoon in one hand and the cup full of medicine in the other. The ridiculous tiny brown hen was walking slowly away.

At that point, Grandma came striding into the yard. From her enormous height, she glared down at the three people below her and shouted, "What's going on around here? Why hasn't anyone brought me my morning cup of tea? It's bad enough having to sleep in the yard with the rats and mice, but I'll be blowed if I'm going to starve as well! No tea! No eggs and bacon! No buttered toast!"

"I'm sorry, Mother," Mrs. Kranky said. "We've been terribly busy. I'll get you something right away."

"Let George get it, the lazy little brute!" Grandma shouted.

Just then, the old woman spotted the cup in George's hand. She bent down and peered into it. She saw that it was full of brown liquid. It looked very much like tea. "Ho-ho!" she cried. "Ha-ha! So that's your little game, is it! You look after yourself all right, don't you! You make quite sure *you've* got a nice cup of morning tea! But you didn't think to bring one to your poor old grandma! I always knew you were a selfish pig!"

"No, Grandma," George said. "This isn't . . ."

"Don't lie to me, boy!" the enormous old hag shouted. "Pass it up here this minute!"

"No!" cried Mrs. Kranky. "No, Mother, don't! That's not for you!"

"Now *you're* against me, too!" shouted Grandma. "My own daughter trying to stop me having my breakfast! Trying to starve me out!"

Mr. Kranky looked up at the horrid old woman and smiled sweetly. "Of course it's for you, Grandma," he said. "You take it and drink it while it's nice and hot."

"Don't think I won't," Grandma said, bending down from her great height and reaching out a huge horny hand for the cup. "Hand it over, George."

"No, no Grandma!" George cried out, pulling the cup away. "You mustn't! You're not to have it!"

"Give it to me, boy!" yelled Grandma.

"Don't!" cried Mrs. Kranky. "That's George's Marvelous . . ."

"Everything's George's around here!" shouted Grandma. "George's this, George's that! I'm fed up with it!" She snatched the cup out of little George's hand and carried it high up out of reach.

"Drink it up, Grandma," Mr. Kranky said, grinning hugely. "Lovely tea."

"No!" the other two cried. "No, no, no!"

But it was too late. The ancient beanpole had already put the cup to her lips and in one gulp she swallowed everything that was in it.

"Mother!" wailed Mrs. Kranky. "You've just drunk fifty doses of George's Marvelous Medicine Number

80

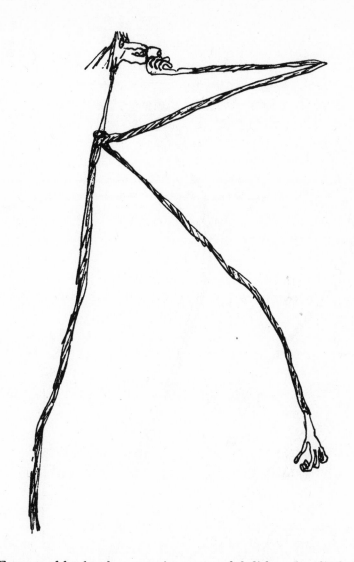

Four, and look what one tiny spoonful did to that little old brown hen!"

But Grandma didn't even hear her. Great clouds of steam were already pouring out of her mouth and she was beginning to whistle.

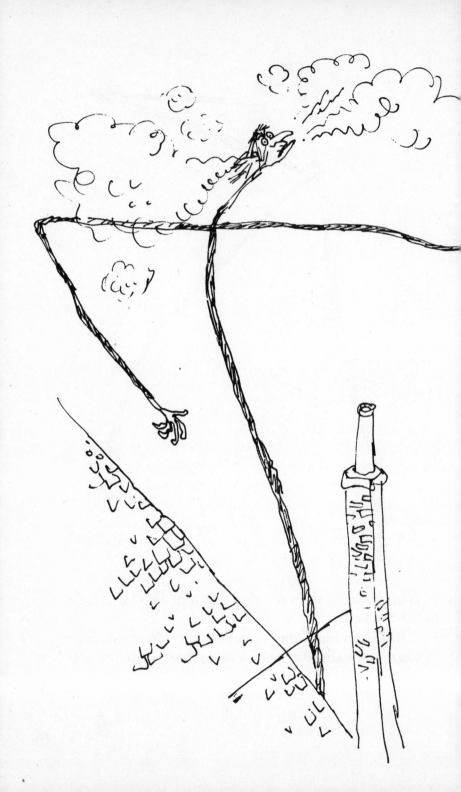

"This is going to be interesting," Mr. Kranky said, still grinning.

"Now you've done it!" cried Mrs. Kranky, glaring at her husband. "You've cooked the old girl's goose!"

"I didn't do anything," Mr. Kranky said.

"Oh, yes you did! You told her to drink it!"

A tremendous hissing sound was coming from above their heads. Steam was shooting out of Grandma's mouth and nose and ears and whistling as it came.

"She'll feel better after she's let off a bit of steam," Mr. Kranky said.

"She's going to blow up!" Mrs. Kranky wailed.

"Her boiler's going to burst!"

"Stand clear," Mr. Kranky said.

George was quite alarmed. He stood up and ran back a few paces. The jets of white steam kept squirting out of the skinny old hag's head, and the whistling was so high and shrill it hurt the ears.

"Call the fire department!" cried Mrs. Kranky. "Call the police! Man the hoses!"

"Too late," said Mr. Kranky, looking pleased.

"Grandma!" shrieked Mrs. Kranky. "Mother! Run to the drinking trough and put your head under the water!"

But even as she spoke, the whistling suddenly stopped and the steam disappeared. That was when Grandma began to get smaller. She had started off with her head as high as the roof of the house, but now she was coming down fast.

"Watch this, George!" Mr. Kranky shouted, hopping around the yard and flapping his arms. "Watch what happens when someone's had fifty spoonfuls instead of one!"

Very soon, Grandma was back to normal height.

"Stop!" cried Mrs. Kranky. "That's just right."

But she didn't stop. Smaller and smaller she got . . . down and down she went. In another half minute she was no bigger than a bottle of lemonade.

"How d'you feel, Mother?" asked Mrs. Kranky anxiously.

Grandma's tiny face still bore the same foul and furious expression it had always had. Her eyes, no bigger now than little keyholes, were blazing with anger. "How do I *feel?*" she yelled. "How d'you *think* I feel? How would *you* feel if you'd been a glorious giant a minute ago and suddenly you're a miserable midget?"

"She's still going!" shouted Mr. Kranky gleefully. "She's still getting smaller!"

And by golly, she was.

When she was no bigger than a cigarette, Mrs. Kranky made a grab for her. She held her in her hands and cried, "How do I stop her getting smaller still?"

"You can't," said Mr. Kranky. "She's had fifty times the right amount."

"I *must* stop her!" Mrs. Kranky wailed. "I can hardly see her as it is!"

"Catch hold of each end and pull," Mr. Kranky said.

By then, Grandma was the size of a matchstick and still shrinking fast.

A moment later, she was no bigger than a pin. . . .

Then a pumpkin seed . . .

Then . . .

Then . . .

"Where is she?" cried Mrs. Kranky. "I've lost her!"

"Hooray," said Mr. Kranky.

"She's gone! She's disappeared completely!" cried Mrs. Kranky.

"That's what happens to you if you're grumpy and bad-tempered," said Mr. Kranky. "Great medicine of yours, George."

George didn't know what to think.

For a few minutes, Mrs. Kranky kept wandering around with a puzzled look on her face, saying, "Mother, where are you? Where've you gone? Where've you got to? How can I find you?" But she calmed down quite quickly. And by lunchtime, she was saying, "Ah well, I suppose it's all for the best, really. She was a bit of a nuisance around the house, wasn't she?"

"Yes," Mr. Kranky said. "She most certainly was."

George didn't say a word. He felt quite trembly. He knew something tremendous had taken place that morning. For a few brief moments he had touched with the very tips of his fingers the edge of a magic world.

AN INTERVIEW WITH
Roald Dahl

This interview, conducted by family friend Todd McCormack, took place in 1988, when Roald Dahl was 71. As Dahl himself said, "I have worked all my life in a small hut up in our orchard. It is a quiet private place and no one has been permitted to pry in there." He not only let Todd McCormack inside the hut, but also gave him rare insight into how he worked, where his ideas came from, and how he shaped them into unforgettable stories. Roald Dahl passed away in 1990, two years after the interview.

WHAT IS IT LIKE WRITING A BOOK?

When you're writing, it's rather like going on a very long walk, across valleys and mountains and things, and you get the first view of what you see and you write it down. Then you walk a bit further, maybe up onto the top of a hill, and you see something else. Then you write that and you go on like that, day after day, getting different views of the same landscape really. The highest mountain on the walk is obviously the end of the book, because it's got to be the best view of all, when everything comes together and you can look back and see that everything you've done all ties up. But it's a very, very long, slow process.

How do you get the ideas for your stories?

It starts always with a tiny little seed of an idea, a little germ, and that even doesn't come very easily. You can be mooching around for a year or so before you get a good one. When I do get a good one, mind you, I quickly write it down so that I won't forget.it, because it disappears otherwise rather like a dream. But when I get it, I don't dash up here and start to write it. I'm very careful. I walk around it and look at it and sniff it and then see if I think it will go. Because once you start, you're embarked on a year's work and so it's a big decision.

How did you get the idea for
James and the Giant Peach?

I had a kind of fascination with the thought that an apple—there're a lot of apple trees around here, and fruit trees, and you can watch them through the summer getting bigger and bigger from a tiny little apple to bigger and bigger ones, and it seemed to me an obvious thought—what would happen if it didn't stop growing? Why should it stop growing at a certain size? And this appealed to me and I thought this was quite a nice little idea and [then I had to think] of which fruit I should take for my story. I thought apple, pear, plum, peach. Peach is rather nice, a lovely fruit. It's pretty and it's big and it's squishy and you can go into it and it's got a big seed in the middle that you can play with. And so the story started.

WHAT IS YOUR WORK ROUTINE?

My work routine is very simple and it's always been so for
the last 45 years. The great thing, of course, is never to
work too long at a stretch, because after about two hours
you are not at your highest peak of concentration, so you
have to stop. Some writers choose certain times to write,
others [choose] other times, and it suits me to start
rather late. I start at 10 o'clock and I stop at 12. Always.
However well I'm going, I will stay there until 12, even if
I'm a bit stuck. You have to keep your bottom on the
chair and stick it out. Otherwise, if you start getting in
the habit of walking away, you'll never get it done.

HOW DO YOU KEEP THE MOMENTUM
GOING WHEN YOU ARE WRITING A NOVEL?

One of the vital things for a writer who's writing a book,
which is a lengthy project and is going to take about a
year, is how to keep the momentum going. It is the same
with a young person writing an essay. They have got to
write four or five or six pages. But when you are writing it
for a year, you go away and you have to come back. I
never come back to a blank page; I always finish about
halfway through. To be confronted with a blank page is
not very nice. But Hemingway, a great American writer,
taught me the finest trick when you are doing a long
book, which is, he simply said in his own words, "When
you are going good, stop writing." And that means that if
everything's going well and you know exactly where the

end of the chapter's going to go and you know just what the people are going to do, you don't go on writing and writing until you come to the end of it, because when you do, then you say, well, where am I going to go next? And you get up and you walk away and you don't want to come back because you don't know where you want to go. But if you stop when you are going good, as Hemingway said…then you know what you are going to say next. You make yourself stop, put your pencil down and everything, and you walk away. And you can't wait to get back because you know what you want to say next and that's lovely and you have to try and do that. Every time, every day all the way through the year. If you stop when you are stuck, then you are in trouble!

WHAT IS THE SECRET TO KEEPING YOUR READERS ENTERTAINED?

My lucky thing is I laugh at exactly the same jokes that children laugh at and that's one reason I'm able to do it. I don't sit out here roaring with laughter, but you have wonderful inside jokes all the time and it's got to be exciting, it's got to be fast, it's got to have a good plot, but it's got to be funny. It's got to be funny. And each book I do is a different level of that. Oh, *The Witches* is quite different from *The BFG* or *James [and the Giant Peach]* or *Danny [the Champion of the World]*. The line between roaring with laughter and crying because it's a disaster is a very, very fine one. You see a chap slip on a banana skin in the street and you roar with laughter when he falls slap on his backside. If in doing so you suddenly see he's broken a leg, you very quickly stop laughing and it's not a joke anymore. I don't know, there's a fine line and you just have to try to find it.

HOW DO YOU CREATE INTERESTING CHARACTERS?

When you're writing a book, with people in it as opposed to animals, it is no good having people who are ordinary, because they are not going to interest your readers at all. Every writer in the world has to use the characters that have something interesting about them, and this is even more true in children's books. I find that the only way to make my characters *really* interesting to children is to exaggerate all their good or bad qualities, and so if a person is nasty or bad or cruel, you make them very nasty, very bad, very cruel. If they are ugly, you make them extremely ugly. That, I think, is fun and makes an impact.

HOW DO YOU INCLUDE HORRIFIC EVENTS WITHOUT SCARING YOUR READERS?

You never describe any horrors happening, you just say that they do happen. Children who got crunched up in Willy Wonka's chocolate machine were carried away and that was the end of it. When the parents screamed, "Where has he gone?" and Wonka said, "Well, he's gone to be made into fudge," that's where you laugh, because you don't see it happening, you don't hear the child screaming or anything like that ever, ever, ever.

How much has living in the countryside influenced you?

I wouldn't live anywhere else except in the country, here. And, of course, if you live in the country, your work is bound to be influenced by it in a lot of ways, not pure fantasy like Charlie with chocolate factories, witches, and BFG's, but the others that are influenced by everything around you. I suppose the one [book] that is most dependent purely on this countryside around here is *Danny the Champion of the World,* and I rather love that book. And when I was planning it, wondering where I was going to let Danny and his father live, all I had to do, I didn't realize it, all I had to do was look around my own garden and there it was.

Roald Dahl on the subject of chocolate:

In . . . seven years of this glorious and golden decade [the 1930s], all the great classic chocolates were invented: the Crunchie, the Whole Nut bar, the Mars bar, the Black Magic assortment, Tiffin, Caramello, Aero, Malteser, the Quality Street assortment, Kit Kat, Rolo, and Smarties. In music the equivalent would be the golden age when compositions by Bach and Mozart and Beethoven were given to us. In painting it was the equivalent of the Renaissance in Italian art and the advent of the Impressionists toward the end of the nineteenth century. In literature it was Tolstoy and Balzac and Dickens. I tell you, there has been nothing like it in the history of chocolate and there never will be.

Roald Dahl, born in 1916 in Wales, spent his childhood in England and later worked in Africa. When World War II broke out, he joined the Royal Air Force and became a fighter pilot. After a war injury, he moved to Washington, D.C., and there he began to write. His first short story was published by *The Saturday Evening Post,* and so began a long and distinguished career.

Roald Dahl became, quite simply, one of the best-loved children's book authors of all time. Although he passed away in 1990, his popularity and that of his many books—*Charlie and the Chocolate Factory, James and the Giant Peach, Danny the Champion of the World,* to name just a few—continues to grow.

Visit www.roalddahl.com to learn more about the author and his books.

✽ ✽ ✽

Quentin Blake has illustrated most of Roald Dahl's children's books as well as many others. The first Children's Laureate of the United Kingdom and a recipient of the Kate Greenaway Medal, Quentin Blake lives in London and teaches illustration at the Royal College of Art.